Nilofer Merchant nails it in this importa...   le
rules to understand that every organization will, ...   le
to deploy. Thankfully, Merchant provides this insightful roadmap
through this new world of business that embraces, openness, stability,
sustainable advantages, profitability, and the new value chain. It's all
here for you to devour. I hope you're hungry."

> – Mitch Joel, Bestselling Author of *Six Pixels of Separation & Ctrl Alt Del*

"A rare combination: strategic, well-researched and actionable. Nilofer
Merchant helps executives see what's at stake in the connection
economy."

> – Seth Godin, Best selling Author, *Purple Cow & Linchpin*

"Social media is not about hooking up line. It's becoming a new
means of production and engagement. Nilofer lays out enormously
helpful 11 rules to embrace the social era."

> – *Don Tapscott, bestselling author of 14 books, most recently Macrowikinomics*

"All companies are social. Business is social. How your brand and
company engage and perform will determine its ability to stay
relevant and profitable. With tools, metrics and markets pulsing with
change, Nilofer's 11 rules are a vital compass. Embrace them."

> – *Lisa Gansky, Entrepreneur & Author of, best seller The Mesh: Why the Future of Business is Sharing*

"Nilofer Merchant has a knack for being able to understand what's
going on in real-time. Following up the New How she argues that
traditional strategic thinking is akin to a well-run bankruptcy. She
offers not just a name (Social Era) to these confusing and turbulent
times but thoughtful and straightforward advice about how both
institutions and people can thrive, not just be the one last standing.
This book is full of contemporary examples, and pointed criticisms
of sacred cow-like organizations and thinking. Required reading for
today's and tomorrow's leaders."

> – Barry Z. Posner, PhD, Co-author of BestSeller: The Leadership Challenge: How to Make Extraordinary Things Happen

"A rare combination: strategic, well-researched and actionable. Nilofer Merchant helps executives see what's at stake in the connection economy."

> — Seth Godin, Author, Meatball Sundae

"Every CEO, CMO and decision maker on the future of a brand needs to read this."

> — Tara Hunt, Founder, Buyosphere & best-selling author of The Whuffie Factor.

"You're missing the whole point when it comes to social media. This isn't about how to get more people to buy your stuff. This isn't even about 'media' anymore. Welcome to 11 Rules For Creating Value in the Social Era. Nilofer Merchant nails it in this important and timely book. 11 simple rules to understand that every organization will, undoubtedly, struggle to deploy. Thankfully, Merchant provides this insightful roadmap through this new world of business that embraces, openness, stability, sustainable advantages, profitability, and the new value chain. It's all here for you to devour. I hope you're hungry."

> — Mitch Joel, President, Twist Image, Bestselling Author, Blogger & Podcaster, Six Pixels of Separation

Nilofer Merchant is a genius. In 'The Social Era,' she deftly dissects the industrial traditions that have brought our business practices to where we are today, and moves on to explain with ease and clarity why they are failing us. Not content to simply describe the state of affairs, she also offers comprehensive, prescient guidelines for taking the future into our own hands. 'The Social Era' opened me up to a whole new way of thinking about business, influence and power.

> — Deanna Zandt, media technologist & author, "Share This! How You Will Change the World with Social Networking"

Pay attention to Nilofer Merchant. And Move over Michael Porter. Modern strategy ain't modern any more.

> — Dave Gray, author, Gamestorming and The Connected Company

"Traditional Strategy is dead, RIP. But do not fear - Nilofer Merchant shows how your organization can thrive with the new Rules of the Social Era. Buy yourself a copy -- as well as every member of your board."

> — Charlene Li, Best Selling Author of "Open Leadership", co-author of best-seller Groundswell, and Founder of Altimeter Group

11 Rules for Creating Value in
the Social Era

NILOFER
MERCHANT

11 Rules for Creating Value in the Social Era

Harvard Business Review Press • Boston

Contents

1. Traditional Strategy Dies

Traditional Strategy, who played a significant and meaningful role in how organizations operated to win in the industrial era, perished on Tuesday, in Boston.

He was forty-three.[1] The cause of his demise was the numerous complications arising from a collision with the Social Era, the context for business in the twenty-first century.

Traditional Strategy (T.S.), born of Joseph Schumpeter and Frederick Winslow Taylor, combined capitalism and industrial efficiency. T.S. had a rich and full life, contributing significantly to the era of big business. For nearly four decades, he was anointed by leaders to guide and inform business organizations and society at large through the dynamics of corporate strategy, industry influences, advantage, market power, and competitiveness. He established position and identified which markets to pursue, as well as ways to design and maintain competitive advantages, and, finally, to defend against competitors. He fueled scale, efficiency, and productivity.

He leaves behind a signature accomplishment: each organization was

---

[1] I'm talking about the business strategy currently in use today, first introduced in the 1970s. I don't like the term it is often referenced by, *modern strategy*, since it is anything but.

encouraged to be unique, to carve out its own differentiated identity, to set itself apart from its rivals. While not all organizations understood or truly adopted this philosophy, T.S. did foster the understanding that strategy is all about making choices and trade-offs, and deliberately choosing to be different. This understanding continues to be highly relevant and, in that, the legacy of T.S. will live on.

T.S. was a central figure in the industrial era, when centralized big institutions were the best way to provide scale. While his beliefs may strike many today as outdated, at the time they were considered the cutting edge of business thinking. His legacy includes:

1. **Right strategy reigns supreme**. A group of elite executives once designed the highly considered and analytically rigorous "right" strategy and then handed it over—apparently via a program called PowerPoint—to managers and their underlings to execute it. This worked well in a simpler time when markets were stable, and when information was scarce and staff needed to be told exactly what to do. Back then, mobilizing the talent and creativity of *all* members was not required to be competitive. In T.S.'s lifetime, markets evolved at a leisurely pace—the speed at which a teenager moves in the morning—so businesses could take their time to consider "the" right response to a new opportunity or threat. The idea that there could be many possible right responses, and that a business could try them concurrently and experimentally, would not take hold for several more decades. And far too few organizations recognize that more than a winning idea, it is important to engage the hearts and minds of their highly educated workforce.

2. **Size matters**. Size created competitive barriers and correlated with market power. Being big allowed organizations to corner the means of production and negotiate lower raw-goods supply costs, giving leverage and pricing power. Big dollars also bought vital access to once-limited media outlets. This meant some dominant firms could reach consumers when others could not, and thus lock out potential competitors. Taken together, these norms supported a mind-set in which size could protect the firms—or at least buy time. Being big had many advantages and no meaningful disadvantages. Size came

to be its own measure of success.

3. **Stability rules**. During T.S.'s lifetime, economic disruptions were thought to be exceptions. It thus made sense to invest in building organizational structures to last. Minimizing variability was seen as essential, which resulted in the hallmarks of the T.S. organization: top-down command and control, division of labor into parsed work, and standardized routines. Predictability was programmed into the business model. Following that embedded logic, the leader's role often centered on optimizing systems and processes around the organizational structure so that people could continue to do what they did yesterday, only more efficiently. Although the idea that disruptions are rare may seem quaint in today's world, vast numbers of organizations are still functioning under the assumption that change is the anomaly, rather than the norm.

4. **Sustainable advantages exist**. T.S. taught us that industries consist of relatively enduring and stable competitive forces that, once understood and exploited, can provide the firm with a long-lasting advantage. Yet, the lifespan of companies listed in the Standard & Poor's index has steadily declined over the last forty years, suggesting the limitation of that idea. We set an annual strategy and then spend most of the year executing against that strategy. Reviewing Traditional Strategy before the appropriate next cycle is then interpreted by corporate boards as an execution problem—such as trying to move the goal posts. This has created a false tension for many organizations—do we focus on the current business and market, or do we build the capacity to identify and tap into the next?

5. **The customer is the guy at the end of the value chain**. The value chain—as it had been interpreted—meant that organizations directed their efforts at a customer outside the perimeter. The organization made things and told the buyer that it was good, and the buyer bought. But by the 1980s, buyers became customers with cynicism, opinions, and expectations, and by the 1990s, the old approach was starting to show the strain. Then in the early twenty-first century, so-called "customers" began to exert co-creative tendencies. During this time T.S. underwent his first major hospitalization; his legacy that

the idea that products can be co-created is still often treated as an anomaly. Even in these enlightened times, most organizations have a hard perimeter wall between the company and its employees, and the customers.

In the twentieth century, T.S. had a huge impact on how organizations conceived of their work; he has unfortunately also cast a long shadow into the twenty-first. No self-respecting business today should be without a strategy. But it is simply wrong for leaders of organizations to continue to rely on him and his many passé ideas. Though we honor the value he once created, his demise means that organizations have an opportunity to conceive anew the way to create value—from strategy, scale, organizational design, advantage, and production—and to identify the new rules to win.

T.S. is survived by two generations: his immediate children, the management thinkers who are now struggling to fit relatively newer concepts like crowdsourcing, open innovation, transparency, co-creation, and collaboration into its classic models; and his many grandchildren attending business schools who continue to be taught his antiquated ideas from out-of-date textbooks.

Services will be held shortly. In lieu of flowers, you are asked to consider what the Social Era means to you, your organization, and the economy at large.

2. **Rules of the Social Era**

Things we once considered opposing forces—doing right by people and delivering results, collaborating and keeping focus, having a social purpose and making money—are really not in opposition. They never have been. But we need a more sophisticated approach to understand business models where making a profit doesn't mean losing purpose, community, and connection. Finding the right balance among them is key. We will find that balance as we shape new constructs for business models, strategies, and leadership. What we can create will be rich in many senses of the word.

In this book, *11 Rules for Creating Value in the Social Era*, I will cover a lot of ground in what follows—how to create value, how to lead, and even how to hold ideas in the world. But before we dive in, I want to give you the bottom line on what we're going to cover. Figure 2-1 is a quick visual summary of the case studies I'll discuss later.

And, here are the Social Era rules that allow *both* people and institutions to thrive:

1. **Connections create value.** The Social Era will reward those organizations that realize they don't create value all by themselves. If

Area	Traditional	Social Era Business Models	Example
HR	Employees	Curators / Co-Creators	Singularity University
Service	Call Centers	Peer Communities	McAfee
Capitalization	A Few Big Investors	Crowdfunding	KickStarter
Product	Mass Production	Custom Production	Desktop Factory
Distribution	Partnership Contracts	Open Marketplaces	Etsy
Supply Chain	Middlemen with Warehouses	User-Driven Production	Lego Factory
Sales	Sales Team Incentives	Customer Love	Evernote
Marketing	Big Budget	Passionate Users	TED/TEDx

the industrial era was about *building* things, the Social Era is about *connecting* things, people, and ideas. Networks of connected people with shared interests and goals create ways that can produce returns for any company that serves their needs.

2. **Power in community**. Power used to come largely through and from big institutions. Today power can and does come from connected individuals in community. Power can come from the way you work with others, such as one party offering a platform to the multitude of creators. When community invests in an idea, it also co-owns its success. Instead of trying to achieve scale by all by yourself, we have a new way to have scale: scale can be in, with, and through community.

3. **Collaboration > control**. Organizations that "let go at the top"—forsaking proprietary claims and avoiding hierarchy—are agile, flexible, and poised to leap from opportunity to opportunity, sacrificing short-term payoffs for long-term prosperity. No longer can management espouse the notion that good ideas can come from everywhere, while actually pursuing a practice in which direction is owned by a few. No one will tolerate an ''Air Sandwich'' in the organization, where debates, trade-offs, and necessary discussions are skipped.

Instead of centralized decisions, there is distributed input, decision making, *and* distributed ownership.

4. **Celebrate *onlyness*.** The foundational element starts with celebrating each human and, more specifically, something I've termed *onlyness*. Onlyness is that thing that only one particular person can bring to a situation. It includes the skills, passions, and purpose of each human. Onlyness is fundamentally about honoring each person, first as we view ourselves and second as we are valued. Each of us is standing in a spot that no one else occupies. That unique point of view is born of our accumulated experience, perspective, and vision. Some of those experiences are not as "perfect" as we might want, but even those experiences are a source of ideas and creativity. Without this tenet of celebrating onlyness, we allow ourselves to be simply cogs in a machine—dispensable and undervalued.

5. **Allow all talent.** "Doing work" no longer requires a badge and a title within a centralized organization. Anyone—without preapproval or vetting or criteria—will create and contribute. And this fundamental shift changes how any organization creates value, and how many individuals gather together—much like gazelles organize into a herd. This talent inclusion—across ages, genders, cultures, sexual orientation—is essential for solving new problems as well as for finding new solutions to old problems. Be the one to enable that connected individual in your enterprise, through systems and leadership, and you win.

6. **Consumers become co-creators.** More and more companies embrace consumers as "co-creation" partners in their innovation efforts, instead of as buyers at the end of a value chain. Consumers, traditionally considered as value exchangers or extractors, are now seen as a source of value creation and competitive advantage. This collaboration shares power between the participants as we start to recognize value creation as an act of *exchange*, not simply a one-way transaction. As an exchange, all parties need to do it sustainably as each must have equilibrium to stay viable.

7. **Mistakes can build trust.** Reach and connection in the Social Era start to be understood as a relationship similar to `falling in love`,

following an arc of romance, struggle, commitment, and co-creation. These are not easily controlled by one party over the other but are a process of coming together. And the relationship gains strength from trying new things and the resulting failures, for it is in the process of making mistakes—and the ensuing forgiveness—that resilience develops. Any vulnerability we feel along the way actually begets trust in the marketplace. And though they are difficult to forge, such robust relationships are more likely to endure the inevitable ups and downs of the market.

8. **Learn. Unlearn. (Repeat.)** Rather than viewing change as an aberration, we understand it as a natural part of the organization's development. Adaptability is central to how organizations and people thrive in the Social Era. In psychological language, the key to adaptability and personal growth is *resilience*. In biology, the equivalent term for adaptive skills is *plasticity*. In financial language, the term we might have used in the industrial era was liquidity, because it could measure how an organization was able to withstand the unexpected. In the Social Era, the term to use is *flexibility*. Our goal is to learn our way into the future. Instead of viewing strategy as a set end point, it becomes a horizon to aim for. Instead of asking employees to each simply man their own oar, we must encourage their capacity to navigate, to tack and adapt as conditions shift. Instead of perfection and getting it right the first time, innovation can be continuous, and core rather than episodic.

9. **Bank on openness.** Protecting intellectual property allows a company to keep its edge, to erect barriers to entry from competitors, to establish entirely new markets. At least, it used to. Then along came the Social Era, with its networks through which open, connected ideas became powerful, even catalytic. It's the difference between holding our ideas in a tight, closed fist or holding out our hand, open to what happens next. We might imagine that if we hold an idea tight enough, we'll end up with a diamond. But when we hold open an idea as if in an open hand, we are unlocking the vault of limitless human capabilities to create new and better ideas that are owned together.

10. **Social purpose unleashes ownership**. The social object that unites people isn't a company or a product; the social object that most unites people is a shared value or purpose. Purpose is a better motivator than money. Money, while necessary, motivates neither the best people nor the best *in* people. Purpose does. When people know the purpose of an organization, they don't need to check in or get permission to take the next step; they can just do it. In that world, purpose *and* community are integral to what and how they create value. Nonprofits, causes, and similar organizations have leveraged the power of people and purpose for years. (Having little or no money, they had to.) But business hasn't been able to see the upside of purpose. With social purpose, alignment happens without coordination costs. Social purpose makes customers and team members more than transactions and payroll recipients. It allows people to "tear down that wall" between who is "inside" and "outside" the firm, creating a more permeable organization that unleashes the inherently collaborative nature of work—like a herd of gazelles running leaderlessly, daringly, across a plain.

11. **(There are no answers.)** While these are the working notions of the Social Era rules, the key is to figure out how to create value in a demanding, ever-changing market. Don't assume any set of rules is fully baked. Accept that your job is to stay alert to what happens next to figure out what assumptions need to be tuned. Listen, learn, adapt.

Let's dive in.

3. Shift Forward

A Google executive: "This business model is right for a company selling Purina Dog Chow, circa 1970." A Cisco executive: "There's no way we could *ever* be this collaborative."

Obvious, or unachievable? When we're talking about reorganizing for a fast, fluid, flexible way of doing business, the responses to the new rules seem to fall sharply on one side or the other.[1]

The companies thriving today are operating by a new set of rules. Companies like REI, Kickstarter, Kiva, Twitter, Starbucks—they get it. They live it. And to them, notions like distributing power to everyone, working in community to get things done, or allowing innovation to happen at all

---

[1] In 1997 *Wired's* editor, Kevin Kelly, wrote a story called "New Rules for the New Economy." His focus was on networks, the "thickening web" that was forging a different set of connections, and perhaps even a source of catalytic power. Many of his then "radical" rules have become commonplace truths for the companies thriving in what I've labeled the Social Era. Two of them are just coming into their own and are foundational to the thesis of *11 Rules for Creating Value in the Social Era.* Connected people with shared interests and goals, he argued, create "virtuous circles" that can produce returns for any company that serves their needs. And organizations that "let go at the top"—forsaking proprietary claims and avoiding hierarchy—will be agile, flexible, and poised to leap from opportunity to opportunity, sacrificing short-term payoffs for long-term prosperity. Since Kelly wrote his article, towards the end of the 20th twentieth century, these forces have flourished. (And yes, he did inspire the title of this book.)

levels are, well, ridiculously obvious. But too many major companies—Bank of America, Sports Authority, United Airlines, Best Buy, and Walmart—that need to get it, don't. These organizations—all of which I'll talk about later—and others continue to follow the operating rules and ethos of Traditional Strategy. They haven't seen the obituary. This is why organizations that think their status as an "800-pound gorilla" gives them an edge are struggling to survive, let alone thrive.

Too many still see social as the purview of two functions: marketing and service. It's either "Like us on Facebook!" or "We're so sorry you're having a problem." While a few have figured out that they can use social to listen to the market—sort of like putting a stethoscope to the market heartbeat—there is more to this social thing.

But before we can explore it, we need to disaggregate two words—*social* is not always attached to the word *media*. Social can be and is more than marketing or communications-related work.

These 800-pound gorillas are feeling the Social Era all around them, but are failing to notice how significant a change it has produced. Perhaps that is because it has shown up in bits and pieces, sometimes wrapped up in technology whiz-bang-ness. You might have seen it arrive via freemium models, crowdsourcing, online communities, virtual workforces, social networks, co-working locations, and so on. Each of these on its own is interesting but not the central idea; each on its own is only an example of how value is created *with* others, allowing seemingly disparate individuals to create value in a way that once only centralized organizations could.

When we look at all the parts *together*, we can see how it affects *everything*.

Yet, it would be easy, if someone had an already-successful enterprise to run (or even a struggling one to resurrect), to miss how much the overall context has changed for the way value is created. The reasons that firms first had leverage—economies of scale and information efficiency—have changed.[2] The Social Era dramatically decreases the cost of communication

---

[2] According to Ronald Coase, people begin to organize their production into firms when the transaction cost of coordinating work through the existing market exchange, given imperfect information, was greater than what you could do through a centralized organization. (source: Wikipedia). The solution has been to gather people together into and within organizations to do something "at scale."

(e.g., finding people and collaborating with them), changing one of the fundamental reasons that centralized scale could create strength. We're at an inflection point where we can see that some early social components add up to more than tools, information-enabled efficiency, products, services, or processes. It is not that we have *more* ways to be social, it is that the net difference of all these different ways to be social allows for the ability to scale in an entirely new way—through and with connected individuals. Clay Shirky, in his book, *Here Comes Everybody*, says the social urge to share isn't new, but that before, the hurdles to do so were so big that it couldn't happen easily. The improvement in what is possible creates new economic effects of increased socialness that add up to a new business model, which is the way an organization creates, delivers, and captures value. They also shift the ethos by which we lead and work.

It's helpful to call this new context the *Social Era* to emphasize a point: while in the industrial era, organizations became more powerful by being bigger, in the Social Era, companies can also be powerful by working with others. While the industrial era was about making a lot of stuff and convincing enough buyers to consume it, the Social Era is about the power of communities, of collaboration and co-creation. In the industrial era, power was from holding what we valued closed and separate; in the Social Era, there is another framework for how we engage one another—an open one. In this framework, powerful organizations look less like an 800-pound gorilla and more like fast, fluid, flexible networks of connected individuals— like, say, a herd of 800 nimble gazelles.

Here's the simplest way to define the Social Era: the industrial era primarily honored the institution as a construct of creating value. And the information age (inclusive of Web 1.0 and Web 2.0 phases) primarily honored the value that data could provide to institutional value creation. It allowed for greater efficiency to do the same things that were done in the industrial era. The Social Era honors the value creation starting with the single unit of a connected human. That shift in focus has profound implications for business, and those implications are the subject of this book.

The exact parameters of this shift are still underway and rapidly evolving. It would be foolish to suggest that a few years into a new era, we're all clear on exactly where we're going and what is going to happen. I'm much more interested in what business can *do* about these shifts, which is why I'm trying to capture the early qualitative direction. In my experience, first working for Apple, then GoLive (bought by Adobe) and Autodesk, being an entrepreneur and adviser to many Fortune 500 organizations, advising start-ups at Stanford University, and now as a corporate director, I understand something important: if we wait until we can document the shift with a 10-year longitudinal study, most of the companies we know and work with—perhaps yours—will be gone.

You might wonder why I'm not using Enterprise 2.0 (E2.0) or social business (#socbiz) terminology. Enterprise 2.0 primarily focused on the tools necessary to create information flow, based on the idea that we can do better if we share information freely. Social business (#socbiz) was a term first created by Mohammed Yunus, but more recently has been a popular way to describe the way companies function and generate value for *all* the constituents (stakeholders, employees, customers, partners, suppliers)—the idea being that we add a social overlay to the existing structural framework. Here, I pose a new question with the notion of Social Era: *in what ways can we structure things entirely differently* to create more value in the context of our times, to be fast to market, to be fluid in mind-set, to be flexible in how we organize, deliver, and create value?

In the Social Era, organizations can do things entirely differently if we let social become the backbone of their business models. At the organizational level, we will shift from hierarchies to networks and thus free "work" from "jobs" (the subject of chapters 4–7). At a human level, power will be distributed instead of centralized in the hands of a few (chapter 8), which will allow groups to self-organize through shared purpose (chapter 9). At a philosophical level, this will mean a shift from closed and separate approaches to open and connected ones (chapter 10). At a symbolic level, the shift is from being the 800-pound gorilla to a herd of 800 gazelles, where communities—made up of singularly unique individuals—create value.

Despite the provocative first chapter, this thesis is not meant to be exclusionary, meaning the old constructs completely die, replaced entirely by a new set. Yes, some frames are outdated, but this set of ideas needs to be considered as on par with old constructs. For instance, I will argue that where power was once mostly centralized, power can be equally shared, but I still believe there is a place for centralized power. Rather, we have an expanded frontier: ways to create value such as how a McDonald's or Exxon does *and* ways to create value as how a PatientsLikeMe, Etsy, or Kickstarter does.

Now some of you might be skeptical of this idea. And you would be in good company. After I first wrote about this thesis on *Harvard Business Review*'s blog, some leaders of Fortune 500 organizations—the 800-pound gorillas of their markets—called. One was the chairman of a major bank, another the CMO of a nationwide retail firm, another the corporate director of a huge insurance product company.

All were interested in what the Social Era could mean for their businesses. But within minutes, all these conversations came down to the same fundamental question. It went something like this: "I agree that things that need to change . . . but does any of this social stuff actually scale?"

As in: How would "co-creating" work across a global supply chain? How would community work across some one thousand stores? How transparent can you really be when there are billions of dollars at stake? What are the success metrics? How long will it take? And, what is the ROI?

These are good questions, and I understand that any organization has to think of how to avoid one-off solutions. There are performance numbers to hit and growth to manage. Scale is necessary to give innovation impact.

But here's the problem with asking, "does it scale?" as the first question: before you can know if it scales, first you have to know what "it" is. When I asked each of these successful and very smart executives that question— "What does the application of these Social Era Rules look like, for you?"— they had no answer. These leaders, however well intentioned, have started with the wrong question. (Now you know why I left out their names when I first started the story.) By asking first, "does it scale?" they have skipped past the more important question, which is, "what could *it* be for us?"

A friend of mine who runs a venture capital firm in Silicon Valley suggests to me that the gorilla versus gazelles tension is an issue of big versus small. He tells me to ignore the big enterprises, that they are not the future; instead, he says, focus on start-ups, which are naturally gazelle-like to begin with. It reminds me of Joseph Schumpeter, the noted economist, saying in 1909 that small companies were more inventive than large ones. But I'm not willing to give up on large firms. (And in fact, in 1942, Schumpeter reversed himself and argued that big companies had more incentive to invest in new products.) Today, people assume that small companies are creative and big firms are slow and bureaucratic, but I think both are oversimplifications. The key is to figure out how to consistently create value in a demanding, ever-changing market. That is hard no matter what size you are. It is not enough to have start-ups act gazelle-like in their early formation but then get lethargic and stuck as they age because they follow the rules of T.S.

I believe we can get the 800-pound gorillas of our day to act more like nimble gazelles—fast, fluid, flexible. It's not that we'll do what we did yesterday a little faster. We will not tweak our way to the new. It will be wholly insufficient to put the word *social* in front of existing business models and expect things to change. Instead, we need to reimagine the enterprise for the Social Era. We need to use business models that will allow connected humans with shared interests and goals to work together to produce returns.

Thus far, organizations have been focused on tacking social elements onto their current operations. Social has been adopted programmatically, rather than strategically. Use a community here, consider doing a freemium strategy there, and then, of course, engage on Twitter. All that has done is get our old models to move a little faster, and they (and our organizations) are straining with the effort of maintaining that speed. It doesn't allow them to actually be fast, fluid, and flexible even though that is what market conditions warrant.

Before diving into the specifics, I want to point out the macro-shifts you'll see along the way.

1. **Scale can be achieved through communities**. You can create value through openness. Here's an example from technology. Most organizations used to do their own development. Within the last ten years, open source software went from being a programming lark that organizations like Oracle or Microsoft made fun of to one that is the default choice for corporations from IBM to Google. Even Microsoft has found a way to open

its Xbox Kinect controller so it can be a `platform for artists and roboticists`. As a result, the platform contributions have far surpassed what Microsoft could have created alone.

Openness is more than "open source"—it is a way to engage ideas.

The value created by platforms that enable many people to contribute can surpass the value created by organizations trying to control each piece. What is created by individuals (without pre-approval, or vetting, or even by defining the exact outcome) can both surprise and delight. Instead of companies trying to achieve scale by all by themselves, scale can be achieved through community.

2. **Consumers can be sources of value creation**. Fifteen years ago, *The Cluetrain Manifesto* was prescient when it taught us that markets are conversations, and that was a great starting point. "Conversations" can go deeper if an organization allows them to become central to how you work, rather than leaving them on the perimeter. How many companies have figured out how to shift from old-school "supply chain management" to the more modern idea of capturing insights and integrating them directly into product design, distribution, and delivery? Because *that's* the point. Instead of a buyer at the end of a value chain, more and more companies are embracing consumers as "co-creation" partners in their innovation practices. This collaborative model fundamentally shares power, improves speed, and shifts the value equation.

3. **Purpose can become an alignment system**. When companies think of social media, they hope to get consumers to "like" them or "fan" them, as if that increased connection is meaningful. Again, that captures the marketing aspect but completely misses the strategic point. *The social object that unites people isn't a company or a product; the social object that most unites people is a shared value or purpose.* When consumers "love" Apple, they are saying they love great design and the shared idea that "thinking differently" is valuable. By "loving" Firefox, the Web community is saying that it believes an open Web browser is valuable to the world. By loving TEDx, a volunteer army of people is saying it believes that smart ideas that get people to think more about their world is a cause worth putting energy into.

Collaborating with people through social purpose creates

advantage because it allows everyone to work toward shared goals. When people know the purpose of an organization, they don't need to check in or get permission to take the next step; they just create value. When people know the purpose, they are not waiting to be told what to do. With social purpose, alignment happens without coordination costs. Social purpose makes customers and team members more than transactions and payroll recipients. It allows us to "tear down that wall" between who is in or outside the firm, creating a more permeable organization that unleashes the inherently collaborative nature of work—like a herd of gazelles running leaderlessly, but in perfect unison, across a plain. Social purpose is a fundamental way to create value in the Social Era.

These shifts mean that, in the Social Era, we have the ability to re-constitute value. *Reconstitute.* That word implies that we can disaggregate the components and remix them as needed. Like having units that can be formed and reformed into the functional construct that works best. Each of the component pieces matters. And so does the formation of how they come together. Each unit's ability to be connected is central to how the value is created. Most importantly, what value creation looks like for any one organization is not the same as what it would look like for another organization. (It is not the same with traditional methods, so why would it be any different with social variables?)

How does this work? What are the rules? What does it mean for all parts of your business?

What follows in chapters 4–6 are some new value levers for the Social Era business model:

- How does social affect how we organize our resources to create value?
- Second, how does *social* influence what we create and distribute to deliver value?
- Third, how does it affect our ability to sell and market to capture value? (While this has been discussed *most* in the Social Era, ideas have not been fully adopted. I'll explain why that is so and what new perspective might be needed.)

From there, I'll discuss what it's like to lead and work in the Social Era; then I'll capture the philosophical "ethos" of the Social Era and finally send you on your way with some exercises to consider what the Social Era can mean for you and your organization.

As you enter this work, I ask that you not judge any of what follows as "right" or "wrong," but ask how much of this could apply, where might this work, and what ways are there to try it out. However much I'd like them to be, these ideas are not 100 percent neat and tidy; they are certainly not a formulaic or even a prescriptive set of ideas. To be perfectly transparent, I have as many questions as answers. So I put this forward as fuel for a richer conversation (in part, because open questions and ongoing conversations are how this era operates). Together, let's challenge assumptions we've all been taught.

What we create in the end will be a different type of organization, one that embodies a culture of constant innovation.

4. Organize

Stanford professor Sebastian Thrun quit his job. But he doesn't plan to go to another prestigious university. Nope. He, like others, has discovered the power of teaching online; in his case, he reached 160,000 students in a single online course. The implications for global education are huge, of course. And that would be interesting on its own.

But there is more to this story than online learning or mass dissemination. This is a central tenet to creating value in the Social Era: what once required a business card, key-card pass, and a title within a centralized organization no longer does. This has implications for organizational design and talent management in firms of all sizes. The freelance revolution, the rise of flextime, the proliferation of virtual teams and offices—all of these trends and more add up to a big shift: "work" is increasingly freed from jobs. Gazelles roam free. This fundamental shift changes how any organization can create value.

This chapter answers the question: if you were going to design an organization from scratch today, what would you design for? And the answer is: flexibility.

Here are two different examples of organizations designed flexibly, at least in one part of their business.

Fluid Model #1: Staffing with "Concentric Circles"

The mark of a good university was to have hired leading-edge researchers into full-time tenured faculty roles, in big buildings. Impressive facilities were a way of showing off the power of wealthy alumni.

Singularity University flips the concept around. "Rather than a locked-down curriculum, full-time faculty, and buildings, we organized for latest thinking, no built-in overhead, and flexibility in design," says Salim Ismail, Singularity's founding executive director. With that design in mind, Singularity delivers three hundred hours of lectures with only seven full-time staff.

The seven full-time employees form a nucleus, or core group, to handle program management, operations, and communications. They also recruit the next rung of talent, ten thought leaders, one for each domain area in which SU teaches. These experts are highly briefed on the purpose and goals of the SU organization. These leaders then act as curators for the rest of the university, assembling ten to twenty domain specialists each, from around the world. Virtual work teams form as needed to coordinate curriculum intersections using Skype and other online tools. While the core group maintains the mission and continuity, the curators act as talent recruiters for the next layer: the extended outer circle of specialized talent that adds topical expertise and content delivery. The talent ratio is 5 percent core, 15 percent curators, and 80 percent specialists. As market needs change, SU is in a unique position to fluidly respond.

Instead of being about organizing in a hierarchical way that focuses on "getting the right people on the bus," this model is about building concentric circles of talent that change and resize as needed. People get on and off the bus, take turns driving, change the bus route: the construct of circles rather than hierarchies allows the organization to tap into a shifting global pool of just-in-time talent.

In 2005, some 30 percent of the US workforce participated in the freelance economy, and some measures suggest it could be as high as 50 percent in 2012, accelerated, in part, by the recession. Some would argue—myself among them—that this number would be larger if portable health care existed. But for organizations the point is that this freelance workforce is not a fad or a trend. And using it fully is a way to design organizations for fluidity and flexibility.

It doesn't just apply to *whom* and *how* we recruit talent. It can change *how* we create value. Model #2 is an example of that.

Flexible Model #2: Customer Service Outside the Perimeter

Typically an in-house cost center, service is usually viewed as a necessary evil and constantly targeted for "efficiency." Over time, notable service firms built outsourcing capacity in India, Malaysia, Singapore, and elsewhere so they could have a global service workforce at a low cost. Support was always tied to a contract with a company to deliver X and Y within certain parameters. Sometimes lost in this process was the expertise that previously came from experienced in-house employees.

McAfee did something transformative to its service exchange by using social. It formed a strong bond of commitment with the hundreds of unpaid technical experts in the larger marketplace who know (and like) McAfee's platform of solutions. It invited these "McAfee Maniacs" to participate in its Web-based technical support. The most prolific Maniacs posted responses numbering in the thousands.

These experts participate for a number of reasons: to keep their skills current, to build a body of work for their own IT support business, and for altruistic purposes. McAfee's competitors were spending between 3 percent and 7 percent of their overall SG&A expenses on service; McAfee's became virtually zero, directly boosting the dollars it could contribute to R&D and other innovation efforts.

Did McAfee or its customers lose something in this change? Hardly. Indeed, McAfee gained a first line of defense—that of loyal, committed experts cooperating in the viability of the platform. Customer satisfaction didn't decline. There is probably no better defense shield than passionate market experts co-opted with a company—and for free.

Isn't This Just Another Way to Cut Costs?

At first, these examples may seem like they're just about reducing direct resources and the related costs.

But it's not just that the 800-pound gorilla is going on a diet of sorts. Organizations take a risk in just running out and trying this, because it is not a model to tack on without understanding the philosophical difference in approach.

The point of these examples is what these organizations *gained*, not what they cut. They gained fluidity and flexibility, important to the demands of the Social Era. But they also gave certain things to the people involved—respect and recognition, shared power, and rewards based on the value brought forward. Sure, there is *less* control, but in exchange for control, they got *more* cooperation and expanded access and shared resources. High performance of the individual and of the organization therefore merges into a common goal when we can enable humans to direct their own lives to create and contribute where they are best suited.[1]

In return, they received, in the case of Singularity, leading content experts coming together to teach current ideas to what they believe are change agents who will make the world better. In McAfee's case, it got experts who passionately solve problems pro bono, just because the connected individuals like doing that work, and because it's their way of making the world better. And McAfee's ability to engage with its community means that it has people deeply interested in making McAfee better, thus building a competitive moat.

These are not stories of *less*; they are fundamentally stories of *more*. The common thread is that the involved participants have a shared purpose, and that creates more power. (I'll spend more time on purpose in chapter 9.)

---

[1] Daniel Pink's bestseller, *Drive*, points to the secret of high performance and satisfaction at work, at school, and at home: the deeply human need to direct our own lives, to learn and create new things, and to do better by ourselves and our world. My point is that organizations can serve this need and themselves at the same time, if they design for it right.

Work Is Freed from Jobs

When there is shared purpose, it doesn't matter how many people work "in the company" and how many people work "with" the company or how many are serving as an army of volunteers who want to advance the mission of the company. What will organizations look like when only 5 percent of talent affecting output is directly on payroll, and others come and go?

Organizations will not need to be big (by themselves), think always in terms of full-time staff, or have a centralized corporate office to have a big impact. They can organize and align outside the conventional thinking of the "perimeter" of an organization. But they will need an extremely clear purpose and shared, decentralized power throughout. When a clear purpose is coupled with shared power, people can self-organize to reach a goal. In essence, Social Era organizations will finally *act* flat (and quite often this leads of speed) because they will actually *be* flat. The artifice of who is in or out of the organization will be less important than what work needs to get done by what talent and with what motivation.

Of course, this affects management's role.

While management has always been about organizing, designing, and maintaining an environment in which individuals work together to accomplish selected goals, the tools at managers' disposal have been rather limited: budget allocation, assignment of responsibilities, hiring and firing. Mostly managers had to focus on doing things that could work at scale. Strategy has said, "do things at scale" and leadership books have said, "bring out the best in people." The Social Era constructs we've been describing say it doesn't have to be about one or the other; we can "allow people to contribute their best" and "create scale" at the same time, as the Singularity University example showed.

And, of course, this is going to require new skills, new metaphors, and surely new tools.[2] Organizations will shift from managing a job

---

[2] Be the one to enable that connected individual in your enterprise through technology systems (and leadership) and you win. You win because this is leveraging all your resources, your human, technical, and organizational resources—what Terri Griffith addressed in her book, *Plugged-In Management*. It's not that you're the most connected, but that you are the most able to thoughtfully connect ideas and people.

function to managing each person based on his or her unique contributions. And individuals will not be thinking about "resume building" but about "portfolio building," as they will come and go to put together a series of projects as "work." This of course raises the bar on individuals to know what they are passionate about in order to come in, perform what is needed, and move on to the next `portfolio` item. Badges will not be about the organization we belong to but the things we care about—our badges of talent and passions and purpose, and the way in which we've built a portfolio of work that demonstrates what we care about.

The bottom line is that work is freed from jobs.

The implications and questions are plenty. Will managers know how to bring out the performance of many individuals who aren't necessarily contributing because of a financial transaction or even in "agreement" of the exchange? When these people come together in multiple units of one, how will leaders enable a way for many to contribute? And how does a leader consider and then determine what is core to his or her firm, and what can and should be done on a project basis? The implication of all of these questions is how these existing distinct roles—as suppliers, employees, contractors, customers—will become less us/them and be more about how people come together to create value in scale.

This changes how we work at the broadest levels, how we structure every single part of our organizations, and how we create value.

5. Deliver

The ability to scale is no longer a function of size. It used to be. But it's not anymore.

Instead, organizations will be measured on different ways they can deliver value. More specifically, how to take in market signals for what customers want, how they want it, where and when they should be able to get it, and how much they are willing to pay. This chapter explores what this looks like in detail.

But first, let's just walk through what has changed in terms of what it took to "deliver value" before and now as it relates to scale:

- *You no longer need to have a "place" to deliver value.* Having a physical presence once provided a real value, being able to find everything you needed in one place. Yet most retailers, including Target and Best Buy, act as storefronts for Amazon, and clearly the value of physical locations is diminishing.
- *You no longer need to have a budget to deliver value.* Bigger companies once had more dollars to buy the mass-market access to consumers back when mass media were the only way to reach an audience. Today, independent producers of almost anything can have marketplaces to reach any audience. Etsy, for example, is a premier marketplace that provides the general public with a way

to buy and sell handmade items. Kitchit is another example of a marketplace that allows you to bring a caterer into your home for an event (substituting for a restaurant meal), and there is a veritable cornucopia of marketplace sites for any particular vertical.

- *You no longer need most functional areas "within" your firm to deliver value.* Gradually, in the name of efficiency, companies figured out how to outsource ever more complex parts of their business. Once-core business functions no longer are—whether that's `service`, with organizations like [24]7 that provide customer service across a range of platforms (Web, mobile, chat, phone), or office space itself, with options like `Regus` or `regional co-working locations` that offer a much lighter footprint to get to work. Human resource management can also be delegated to specialized organizations; payroll and benefits can be managed by `TriNet`; recruitment can be done by `Pinstripe`. Innovations can be incubated and prototyped at `Frog Design`. The results of those prototypes can then be produced in one-off physical production using `computer-aided design and 3-D printing`. An example of such a resource is Desktop Factory, which lets you create toys or sprinkler systems from your 3D printer. The supply chain is managed by any number of `shipping vendors`, whether that's UPS or DHL or FedEx. Accounting tools are in the mix, too. Intuit, Indinero, Mint, and other tools allow accounting to be easily outsourced. Companies need enough financial expertise to be sure they have the capitalization for growth, but lots of compliance and reporting paperwork can be externalized.
- And if they need to raise capital for any of this? Well, they might use Kickstarter or any one of its dozens of imitators. Need to reach customers? Thanks to the Web, the marginal cost of reaching consumers is effectively zero.

In practical terms, here's what all of this means: a person or team anywhere in the world can create scale without being big. That's bad news for the 800-pound gorillas because it fundamentally changes the competitive playfield in unpredictable ways. Where once you could study a marketplace and see a competitor growing in size to be able to compete in your marketplace, a competitor can become viable without giving you any indications and without having to build up their own scaling capabilities.

Most existing organizations—the gorillas—learned their construct via Michael Porter's value chain framework. This model was created pre-globalization, pre-Internet, and certainly pre-Social Era.

So what's left after you take all these parts of the value chain and make them fluid resources to use as needed? The core asset of the organization becomes clear. It is same thing that has always been central to what makes a company great: customer insights and the ability to serve those via its own unique strategy (what only it can uniquely do through a combination of talent, culture, and purpose).

The rest of this chapter is about this notion of customer insights and how value is created in the Social Era, an organization's ability to best respond to them in the way it decides what to make, how much to make, and perhaps how to finance that production.

Social Becomes Central to What We Create, Produce, and Deliver

During Fashion Week in September 2011, Burberry did a direct campaign with everyday consumers (not just the editors and fashionistas) to showcase its new line in what it called a #tweetwalk, letting users tweet about what they liked (or didn't). It created an immediate signal between the company and its users.

It was an interesting first step.

Every brand already has the ability to get direct feedback from consumers on what they like; the friction cost of doing this is effectively zero through a social media conversation. But Burberry stopped short of doing what makes the most sense to its bottom line. Imagine if it had actually created a video of a runway walk that enabled click-to-order. It could produce only what was ordered and thus reverse its supply chain to produce only what is already sold. It could even allow customers to request products in particular colors at premium prices. (By the way, Dell has been doing this for many years and is an early example of social—letting customers drive the supply chain—but today, the modularity of supply chain allows companies to make it more truly customized and less about complicated configurations.) Social gives companies more control to operationally adjust their offers and create zealots by better collecting and amplifying even weak signals.

This puts the customer at the center of the company much more than any lip service about being customer-centric. Ask yourself, what would your production process and systems look like if you were to put customers at the center?

Today, we see brands asking consumers to "like" them on Facebook as a way of getting permission to push information to them. The brand is still the central part of that communication. Imagine what that dynamic becomes when using the "power of pull." This is the term John Hagel and John Seeley Brown coined via their book to capture the notion that attracting and seducing consumers with a relevant, helpful, and unique point of view works better than shoving more messages into the already loud marketplace. But the concept shouldn't just be viewed as an organizing principle for marketing; it can be applied to *all* the ways that value is delivered.

More and more companies embrace consumers as co-creation partners in their innovation efforts, not just as buyers at the end of a value chain.[1] Consumers, traditionally considered as value exchangers or extractors, are now considered a source of value creation and competitive advantage. This collaboration shares power between the participants as we start to recognize value creation as an act of *exchange*, not an extraction. The essence of a good exchange is that each side gets substantially more than what they give up (in their opinions). Co-creation allows for more than a financial exchange but a deeper sense of commitment to the other.

The company's value would be in gathering market signals and using its unique expertise to translate that into customized or right-suited offers.

---

[1] Co-creation describes a trend of jointly creating products. First defined by scholars C. K. Prahalad and Venkat Ramaswamy who introduced the concept in their 2000 *Harvard Business Review* article, "Co-Opting Customer Competence." They developed their arguments further in their book, published by the Harvard Business Press, *The Future of Competition*, where they offered examples, including Napster and Netflix showing that customers would no longer be satisfied with making yes or no decisions on what a company offers. Value will be increasingly co-created by the firm and the customer, they argued, rather than being created entirely inside the firm. And I think it's a fundamental shift in how it creates value.

For example, Lego Factory offered a customized service where consumers could design whatever—their house, their dog, or even their own invented monster—and Lego would make a kit in a program called Design byMe. (Its quality standards were less than it wanted so Lego is currently working on another version of customization.) This program attracted several million people each year to make Lego "theirs."

Of course, social can change what we finance. Here's where the community comes in. You may already know Kickstarter is the largest funding platform for creative projects in the world. Several other platforms exist to allow community to fund expansion. When no one funds you, you know there's no market for your idea. This changes more than the economic source. When a community invests in an idea, it also co-owns its success. In other words, it's not just socially funded; it's socially meaningful. And when products are crowdfunded, the "return" is not just financial.

When people are emotionally invested, they also want to contribute to the value equation.

Manufacturing is also affected. For some time, manufacturing has been offshored to wherever is cheapest. But as speed and customer insights grow in importance, manufacturing will likely return to more local sources. In one such example, a trendy designer recently moved her clothing production to New York. After the move, it took just six weeks to design and deliver a line of leather bags to her stores, rather than the six months it could have taken if the bags had come from Hong Kong.

When companies figure out how to shape their design, production, and manufacturing cycle from rigid planning and production systems to unique customer-driven experiences, they'll design a way to respond in smaller bursts of more profitable cycles.

By allowing customers to directly fund an expansion, companies will know exactly what to build and what is extraneous. By allowing signals to direct production, there's an opportunity to learn immediately what the market responds to. Organizations can be in a constant conversation to learn what is working and what is not, and adapt on the fly. These flexible organizations consistently try new things, adapt to what works, and thus improve the bottom line. What is interesting about this approach is that no company has to get it right the first time; it just has to know how to learn and discover what works for growth.[2] A firm that waits until it gets it right will actually be at a disadvantage.[3]

The gorilla dominated at a time when companies needed and used more capital, and when the value chain could be profit-maximized through vertical integration. To run this traditional organization, leaders had to be focused on being big enough to enable scale, because that's where the profits once were. Once an organization got big, it took a lot to displace it. And for some organizations, like Chevron or McDonald's, this model still applies.

But the Social Era demands something more that is qualitatively different. *The Social Era rewards those that can bring together a herd of gazelles—by which they can be fast, fluid, and flexible. What we reward in the Social Era is being connected to customer insights and acting with relevance in what we produce and deliver.*

This changes things for every type of organization. For example, if Best Buy is going to compete with Amazon, it needs to focus less on having different SKUs from the vendors so they can hide information from consumers. Instead, they need to focus on how to get better signals into their process. For example, consumers might Pinterest desired elements of a home entertainment system they liked, including information about space or noise limitations ("One-bedroom apartment on busy street in New York," or "suburban space that needs stuff protected from little kids"). Then Best Buy or some similar retailer could create a personalized, optimal configuration that the consumer could see in person on a weekend at one of the regional showcases, and then have delivered and set up by service-oriented staff.

This shifts how value creation happens. Once, profits came from vertical integration in the industrial era; power in the Social Era can come from connections, communities, and unlocking the creativity of different parts of the organization. Instead of being the gorilla that dominates others,

---

[2] Rita MacGrath, a leading management thinker, has been saying for some time that it's more important to allow fluidity in an organizational strategy than to get "strategy right."

[3] For several years, Eric Ries, author of *The Lean Startup*, and Steve Blank, author of *Customer Development*, have been showing this concept at work for start-ups. Peter Sims, author of *Little Bets*, talks about making this an innovation muscle any size enterprise should develop.

you can find ways to bring together a herd of gazelles and be more powerful *with* them.

6. **Connect**

It's been over fifteen years since the marketing aspect of *social* first started.[1] So many brilliant people have been writing, speaking, and sharing marketing-related case studies during that time that if I only listed a few, I'd miss some really important thinkers. And if I tried to list them all, I'd hit the word limit on this book. But despite this outpouring of expertise, many organizations still find it ridiculously hard to do (if at all).

This chapter builds on the previous two; I've already discussed how to organize to create value (chapter 4) and how to deliver value (chapter 5). This chapter addresses how the third part of any business model—how you capture value via sales and marketing. The Organize/Deliver/Capture taxonomy is the way many people think of the three parts of the business models. But as you might notice by this chapter title, I think this part of the problem. As Philip Granof recently wrote, marketing has typically used a war metaphor to talk about sales and marketing.

---

[1] It first started with *The Cluetrain Manifesto*, by Rick Levine, Christopher Locke, Doc Searls, and David Weinberger. The book laid out ninety-five principles for communicating with customers. It caused a big stir. Some of the maxims are seriously out of date, some were wrong, but parts of it are just plain brilliant and should be spray-painted on the walls of every organization worldwide. On the ten-year anniversary, Mike Mace—an online expert himself—contributed to an updated commentary on the commandments when he worked for me at Rubicon.

We take *aim* at our *target* market.
We *capture* or *defend* market share
We *seek to gain* shelf space.
We *attack* competition.
We *win* customers.

In the Social Era, the way we complete the third phase of business model is to *connect*.

Some problems are technical, where the solution is finding the best expert in that field and then working to execute her strategy. But other problems require more than an answer to a known question and demand that we spend some energy figuring out whether we're even asking the right question in the first place. Perhaps because marketing has been conceived of as "capture" rather than "connect," we can say that solving what marketing needs to be in the Social Era fits into the second bucket. So, instead of assuming we have answers, let's ask a series of questions about how to achieve reach and connection, in the hopes that we get smarter about the challenge itself.

Does Social Have to Be Chaotic?

The old model for customer relationships—that is, the one still used by many companies today—is built around a buying funnel that progresses from awareness to consideration to purchase to loyalty. Fundamentally, this is an information model in which companies provide the information and customers consume it.

The funnel is a favorite of marketers because it is linear, unidirectional, and transaction-centric. What this means is that there is a single path built around discrete actions by the company and responses from the buyer. It is not hard to determine where any particular consumer is in the process, so tracking and metrics are straightforward and easy to calculate. Where many marketing activities are hard to measure, this one is easy.

Yet the passive, obedient consumer and paternal, in-control organization have given way to a vocal, informed consumer and an organization struggling to comprehend what this all means to its bottom line. (Of course, the notion of a passive consumer was always as misleading as the idea of a "mass market"; consumers were never as passive as companies like to think.)

So social marketing experts will tell you that marketing has to become more conversational, more relationship-oriented. While most companies have now learned how to say hello and how to apologize, I would argue that few have accepted the fact that power has shifted. Power has shifted from a company-centered worldview where it was responsible for figuring out what to create and telling the consumer (loudly and often if it had money to do so) what to buy, to a time when consumers can co-create with one another and with brands. Brands that don't recognize the shift in power use the technological tools but don't act social. Are the persistent tweets that always apologize but never fix the situation really social at all? (I'm looking at you, @united, @att, and @comcastcares.) If that's a "relationship," it's a rather boorish one and one that most of us would abandon.

Social has never been a technology trend, as it is often depicted by the experts. Humans have always wanted to connect, organize, and create value. Back when there were tribes, people had community and naturally had relationships in the marketplace. But our current organizational constructs have been focused on scale at the cost of connection. In truth, if we let it, marketing in the Social Era will look like any other relationship, perhaps like falling in love, following an arc of romance, struggle, commitment, and sometimes, co-creation:[2]

- **Romance**. This first phase is about introductions. In purchasing, as in dating, people don't want to think about big commitments when they are still trying to decide if they even want to get to know you better; this phase of connection is about exploring.
- **Struggle**. As we spend time together and get to know each other, there is a mutual effort to learn how both parties in the relationship are going to fit together. Each person has to realize it's not all about him or her. After all, there needs to be balance if a relationship is going to last for the long term. In the business context, the parallel

---

[2] Harry Max provided the early insight of "falling in love" and the arc. Ever since the idea entered my brain three years ago, I continue to evolve it. Harry incubates great ideas with many people.

holds: both parties have to share in the outcome. For example, a local retailer in my area, Crimson Mim, recently directed me to buy a product online from another vendor because it would better complete my outfit, an experience that is seen by the consumer (me in this case) as generous. Consumers can contribute to the relationship by signaling their needs so that businesses can serve them, or by deciding to buy from companies whose values they support instead of shopping on price alone. For an organization, this can also be about making information available freely, knowing that it may not get picked as the vendor of choice, but the consumer will still get the best choice for her.

- **Commitment**. When the relationship stabilizes, each knows what to expect from the other and cares enough to be there, for better or for worse. While loyalty in a predominantly one-way, transactional exchange is fragile, commitment in a stable, bidirectional relationship is far more robust. You are willing to forgive one another for mistakes. Or to look past small annoyances because the benefit of being committed is worth the trade-offs. Just as we might hope a married couple would stay together through cancer or financial devastation, we hope that the parties in business can weather through the ups and downs that change brings. For example, when Toscanini's ice cream (once deemed the "Best Ice Cream in the World" by the *New York Times*) messed up its taxes a few years back, its passionate community of ice cream lovers donated about $30,000 in one week in a spontaneous bailout.

- **Co-creation**. Just as not all relationships produce children, not all business involves co-creation. But co-creation produces a different level of ownership of both the product and the brand. In this type of relationship, a customer is no longer merely making a transactional purchase, but participating in the act of creating. If, for example, I design a T-shirt for Threadless, or contribute code to an Open Source Initiative, or correct an entry on Wikipedia, I am creating with the organization. If I purchase that smoking hot Burberry jacket that only fifty customers were allowed to order in a custom color, then not only do I love the jacket, I have created something unique with the brand and therefore have ownership with the brand. Kepler's, an independent bookstore near Stanford University, underwent a similar closure and recovery as Toscanini's, but the story went further. Now that community donations have streamed in to save it, the bookstore and its board—composed of community members—are planning to rebuild as a next-generation community literary and cultural center.

No wonder social marketing is so hard to get right. It is as complex as any relationship. And let's remember this: love isn't rational, but a combination of logic and emotional needs. In this construct, relationships certainly aren't predictable. (Try applying any predictive metrics to your love life and see how it goes.) And, as anyone who's ever been in love can attest, it's not a linear path.

To a company, this can feel like pure chaos. There is not a "thing" to manage. The metrics are new, evolving, and unfamiliar, and so they seem unclear. Social marketing still lacks a prescriptive model that one can put on a PowerPoint slide and show to the board of directors. Instead, like a relationship, it is fluid, not formulaic, with a measure of equality between consumer and creator.

Is a Business Built on Volunteers Manageable?

There are plenty of examples in the pages of HBR—along with other publications—of social business models that use volunteers.

One example is that of TED and TEDx. TED has its main conferences (TED in the United States and TEDGlobal in Europe) where people with relatively big wallets gather once a year to hear smart people give short talks, creating "ideas worth spreading." These TEDtalks are released online and allow global participants to share in the spreading of ideas. In June 2009, TED announced a program called TEDx that allows many to organize their own TED-inspired conference.

By doing this, it got a benefit equivalent to a multimillion-dollar marketing budget by enabling a franchise of passionate users to do their thing. Volunteers coordinated events in places as near as New Jersey and as far as Estonia. There was TEDxKibera, held in Africa's largest shantytowns in Nairobi, Kenya. The first two-and-a-half years of TEDx have resulted in 2,500 events in more than 110 countries.

This is social connection. Passionate people are co-creating because they value TED's purpose. The social purpose is not "build TED's brand"; it's "spread good ideas that matter."

While a social approach certainly lowers the financial overhead of the organization to expand on purpose, the question is, at what cost?

Certainly the Komen controversy showed the complexity of the issue. The Susan G. Komen Foundation is a community-based organization involving many who like a grassroots feel to their cause—finding a cure for breast cancer. In 2010, 1.6 million people participated in its regional "Races for the Cure," staffed by over 100,000 volunteers. But when the foundation stopped its donations to Planned Parenthood, an organization that provides 4 million breast exams annually, it turned what many believed to be an apolitical issue into a political one. The community that provided the basis for Komen's success turned on the foundation, as people began to question whether the organization had changed its purpose. In the Komen–community relationship, the community felt as if this was a major breach of trust. So the cost is that when you work with people, you need to take into account their shared ownership.

The bottom line: the more an organization depends on others, the more expectations they need to wrestle with. If people give to a cause, they expect a relationship, not a transaction. There's a fine line between being a volunteer, which implies an asymmetric power balance, and a member of a community, which suggests something more egalitarian. This all evokes many still-unanswered questions, such as: Isn't it dangerous to have so many people believe they co-own the brand? Or, don't these people (at TEDx or McAfee) deserve to be paid for their work? These could lead us to ask, does this model have too many hidden costs?

Can You Make Money This Way?

MySQL became a dominant enterprise software company by "giving away" usage but asking for payment for those that need support and maintenance. There were 6 million users but only five thousand paying customers, just an 0.083 percent conversion rate. Yet that fraction garnered $34 million in revenues, making MySQL an attractive acquisition to Sun Microsystems (and then to Oracle). Similarly, Evernote customers are known for declaring their love for the product as they buy—and buy they do. As the CEO of Evernote says, this approach increases the commitment of the consumer to keep Evernote around. When the relationship is focused on commitment, not transaction (*what have you bought from me lately?*) between consumers and the company, it fundamentally shifts power.

The software and mobile app world is starting to seep into everyday culture. We're starting to see this relational approach—pay me what you think it's worth, after you've used my service or product—in everything from music to food to hairstyling. Where once usage came last, at the end of the marketing process, it is now more frequently starting the cycle.

This shift is perhaps the most terrifying and unpredictable thing any organization can face. This philosophical approach could change every aspect of the business, from product design to engineering to marketing, sales, and support. Sure it sounds good to say, "Pay if you love it," but what if not enough consumers do? Flexibility sounds good as a consumer, but it is terrifying to the brand (and the finance team that creates the budget). The MySQL story shows a razor-thin margin of adoption—and it was one of the successful ones.

So, perhaps many organizations look at this social approach and ask, yeah, but what if not enough people choose *us*? That's a definite risk, but not adapting to the changing phenomena of the Social Era is also a risk.

How Do We Resolve These Conflicts?

We want innovation, but without experiencing failure. We want to embrace the new, but without risk. We want to act fast and fluid, but to maintain tight controls. We want to empower everyone, but retain decision rights for ourselves. We want to experiment, but we also want predictability. We want to be flexible to customer input, but remain ruthlessly efficient. We want to adapt, but we fear the death of familiarity.

This is why it's hard to go from being an 800-pound gorilla to a herd of nimble gazelles; an organization goes from being a centralized institution that competes through overpowering strength and scale to a set of relationships or interrelationships. Gazelles thrive and win by how they share power with one another. And, as a result, they can act fast, fluid, and flexible. For organizations, this is key to winning in the marketplace.

Make no mistake. Marketing in the Social Era is not easy. Being heard above the noise is a true challenge. But reach and connection allow for a different construct.

When customers are central to all we do, they are not easily controlled and they are not predictable. But remember, it is making mistakes—and the ensuing forgiveness—that gives relationships their resilience. This connection might take longer to forge than a transactional exchange, but its outcomes will last longer. Any vulnerability we feel along the way actually begets trust in the marketplace. And though they are difficult to forge, such robust relationships are more likely to endure the ups and downs the market inevitably deals any organization.

7. Capture

I've talked about the levers of value in the Social Era—how social can be used to organize how to create, what to deliver, and the ways to interact in the marketplace.

Specifically, I've drawn three conclusions.

- **Work is freed from jobs**. This means that human resources change when most of the people who create value are neither hired nor paid by you. And competition has changed so that any company can achieve the benefits of scale through a network of resources: for example, designing a product from anywhere, producing it through a 3-D printer, financing it communally, and distributing it from anywhere to anywhere.
- **The value chain has changed**. The customer is no longer just the buyer but also a co-creator. Co-creation, crowdfunding, and customization can lend a deeper value to the pricing.
- **With, not at**. It used to be that capturing value was about hiding price or appearing perfect, when in reality, we return to a truly social construct of how connection happens. Instead of sales and marketing, exchanges follow the arc of relationships: romance, struggle, commitment, and co-creation. Connection supersedes control. Capitalization changes when a community invests in an idea; it also co-owns its

success. In other words, it's not just socially funded; it's socially meaningful, which of course changes the value proposition.

Competition has changed. Value proposition has changed. Work has changed. Yet our business models have not changed to keep pace with these shifts. Until we understand both how these combined factors let social be the backbone of our organizations and how we make money, we're not answering the strategic question: what are the ways the Social Era affects everything we do? This chapter tackles that question: what changes in the business models of the Social Era, and what is the implication for winning in the marketplace?

Shifts in Economic Terms

The insights I just covered in detail in chapters 4 through 6 affect the economic model. They change the cost structures, they change what defines "premium value," and they change how flexibility leads to a different type of competitive advantage.

What I've discussed so far is not transitory or reversible, but fundamental and irrevocable. Remember when Nicholas Carr said IT was a commodity and then people got into a huff? The uproar was deafening for about six months until it became clear that Carr was right. IT cost had decreased and its adoption had increased to the point where IT no longer offered the distinct advantage it had previously.

In the previous chapters, I've described a similar evolution in many once-core business functions, from manufacturing to HR to accounting. Organizations went from needing to build it themselves to having a variety of globally outsourced resources. Organizations no longer need to own everything to create value.

The net effect is that an org chart drawn in the 1990s would have had different parts: engineering, manufacturing, IT, HR, and finance, and each would be drastically different. That same org chart drawn today would be more fluid and flexible—and economically leaner, for sure.

Here are few implications:

- Many fixed costs have become variable costs. And where gorillas also had buying power that kept costs low and distribution to keep volumes up, these levers are no longer as powerful.
- Marginal cost plays a bigger role in the value equation. In many parts of value creation, the marginal cost approaches zero.
- Barriers to entry have fallen. Massive fixed costs, in the form of space, capital equipment, and staff, no longer keep out smaller firms. Size is indeterminate as a threat factor.

The Business Model

Now let's think of what that means in terms of business models in the era of Traditional Strategy:

The value equation from forty years ago would be represented economically as:

$$\text{Profits}_{TSera} = (\text{Margin}) \times (\text{Units sold}) - (\text{Fixed costs})$$

Profits were a function of the advantage of scaled market power. Buying power kept costs low, and distribution power kept volumes up. Massive fixed costs, in the form of space, capital equipment, and the overhead of staff, were a barrier to entry for smaller firms, which kept out new entrants—it just was not profitable to enter the market without scale. This allowed a bigger firm to have both a greater margin and offset its significant fixed costs. Today, size often doesn't lead to pricing power, so margins are under pressure. And with fewer fixed costs, the benefits of scale (through a centralized organization) to the profit line are nominal.

The value equation in the Social Era has very few fixed costs:

$$\text{Profits}_{SE} = (\text{Margin}) \times (\text{Units sold})$$

When we make what was once a fixed cost a variable cost, the minimum profitable unit volume is steadily approaching a unit of one. This doesn't even capture the harder-to-measure benefits of customization, co-creation, and specialization on the value equation.

Reinventing the "How" as a Way to Handle Disruption

In Clay Christensen's iconic work, *The Innovator's Dilemma*, he describes how small newcomers eat off bits of an established leader's business through lower cost structure and a willingness to accept lower margins. This phenomenon has been seen in industry after industry, and it is usually focused on the cost of delivering goods and services. In other words, "Look how the steel mini-mills making rebar disrupt the established integrated steel mills making sheet steel." At each point in the disruption, it makes economic sense for the big company to surrender that bit of the market to the disruptor, so big companies logically put themselves out of business.

An analogous process is going on with the organizational structures of businesses themselves. Aside from market-specific competition from below, there is also competition from disruptive organizations that are finding new ways to get work done. This change is just as threatening to established businesses as the process competitors Christensen identified, and just as difficult to respond to.

Where once the reexamination of an organizational structure happened every decade or so to support a change in the business model, the ability to rapidly reinvent the structure—the *how*—becomes a disruptive skill in itself.

This, in part, kills Traditional Strategy. With Traditional Strategy, it was important to have a right strategy and it was possible to own an advantage for a relatively long time. Thus, you wanted a stable structure to execute a plan once it was put into play. It was expensive to change your mind because you were turning a battleship. And, changing organizational design midstrategy was incredibly risky. In the Social Era, the idea is to get the general direction right and rely on feedback loops to iterate and adjust direction.[1]

---

[1] Chris Argyris's idea of learning organizations has been seminal in how I view work and value creation. If you don't already know of his "double-loop" learning idea, it's worth reading.

In this framework, it is cheap to change your mind, and you don't need to make big commitments; therefore, you set a course, adjust as needed, and learn until you get it right. This is what enables customers to be a part of your business rather than "out there." Having work freed from jobs enables it. And it benefits from the fluidity of design. Course correction in the Social Era is more like a kayak shooting the rapids.

An organization can—and should be—perpetually reinventing its constructs.

How does the structural fluidity lead to disruptive ability?

To answer this question, let's look at Singularity University, which I mentioned earlier. You might recall that it delivers an education curriculum of three hundred hours with seven full-time staff. Its organizational model lets it fluidly reinvent what it creates next, thus baking in innovation with its disruptive design. In particular, some 80 percent of its business resources—the value levers just covered in chapters 4–6—are flexible. So its "how" is very different. But this new "how" also enables a new "what."

The business model allows Singularity University to persistently review "what's the next big thing" and adjust. That's not a realistic option for institutions that have a tenured staff of experts wrapped up in things that were innovative fifteen years ago. Using Christensen's metaphor, educational institutions are the sheet steel—with ever-increasing tuitions to support their tenured staff—while Singular University is the rebar. But its flexible design has become a lever of value and gives it the chance to *keep being* the "new rebar."

Fast, fluid, flexible organizations that are made with this social-era backbone can assess needed changes, be quick to respond, and be nimble in how they assemble people. In net, this lets them quickly address both problems and opportunities in the markets.

Business Models for the Social Era

The Web 2.0 world, with its related efficiencies, was the bridge between the industrial era and the Social Era. This does not mean that every Internet company has an innovative, new, "social" business model. Far from it. For instance, one could argue that Amazon (the book- and product-selling side of the business, not Amazon Web Services) and Netflix are examples of companies that have maximized the efficiencies of the information age but still (largely) operate by the traditional strategy rules. However, Web 2.0 did bring us several new business models:[2]

- **Freemium model**, as the MySQL option showed, where you give away first and create a `conversion funnel` for some users to pay you. This works because the value equation of distributing things online has relatively low marginal cost.
- **Platforms as marketplaces**, as eBay and Amazon have demonstrated. Today, you can find just about anything in discrete online marketplaces. Today there are many marketplaces, already described, such as Etsy and Kitchit.
- `Open business models`. Henry Chesbrough shows that firms can and should use external ideas as well as internal ideas, and internal and external paths to market. Open Source is probably the best iconic example of a way an organization can use a community-made product to enable its own business value. Certainly, we know Xerox, IBM, GE, Intel, and others are using open source as core to their own development process.
- **The Web's efficient way** of letting any size business access consumers means that the advertising-supported models get a lot of visibility through Google and Facebook.
- **Collaborative consumption** points to the declining need to own piles of products (and services); some business models will allow us to share and use things only when needed. In San Francisco, and many other cities where many folks use public transportation for commuting and shopping, few need to own a car. So, there's Zipcar, which allows you to "own" a car for a few days or a month, on an as needed basis. The idea of renting has been around for awhile, but the Web gave us a new way to share (a depreciating asset) for the benefit

---

[2] Bestselling author Alex Osterwalder has written an amazing book entitled the *Business Model Generation*, which simplifies and teaches the components of how to think of your business model—value propositions, channel strategies, pricing approaches, and so on. He's captured both traditional business models and most of the ones created by the information/Web era.

of the earth.[3] Another version of this on the enterprise side was software as a service (SaaS), which allowed people to rent software instead of buying it outright, lowering the capital acquisition cost.

These models are all valuable but only partly social.

Let's face it, every business model has already been done in some form already. Free was around before social. For example, as I was growing up, the local candy store owner would hand out one relatively cheap Lemon Tarts candy to any kid who came in the store, knowing that it would continue to draw a crowd, and some percentage of parents would buy the more expensive product lines. The Web just took an already existing business model (free) and made it easier to do on a broader scale. In the case of software, the Web allowed easier distribution of products (and a lower marginal cost) to enable freemium pricing as a core new business model. The same is true for rental models that were around in the traditional world, as you likely remember from high school prom tuxedos to bowling alley shoes. In the Web 2.0 era, we saw that in SaaS models that allow a lower cost of ownership of software for enterprises. It was just rental with a more efficient cost structure. My point is that *every* business model has already been done in some form already—sponsorship, advertising, free, rental—in the traditional era and the Web era.

The question is really what could any business look like when *all* the business levers are socially oriented; what could happen next? We have yet to see the full range of business models we can create when *all* the levers are exercised. The Social Era, with its fundamentally different ways to create value through connected individuals, will surely bring more options.

We need innovative business models to go hand-in-hand with innovative ideas.[4]

---

[3] Lisa Gansky, author of *The Mesh*, and Rachel Botsman, author of *Collaborative Consumption*, shows how the Web turbo-charges our ability to share. This has created a platform for business models based on community use of expensive objects and services.

[4] Saul Kaplan describes why organizations fail at business model innovation: `http://blogs.hbr.org/cs/2011/10/five_reasons_companies_fail_at.html`. The net is that we spend too much time preserving what is, rather than inventing what is next. In my mind, this thinking is a by-product of believing there is such a thing as a sustainable competitive advantage that will last. Instead, we need to learn to leap from opportunity to opportunity, not hoard and protect the one thing we got right last time.

Importantly, these new constructs will give us more than money. If we can use assets more effectively, we will lower our impact on the earth. If we can find local resources, we can connect to our community in a different way. Maybe this means we will generate more prosperity, not just more wealth. Maybe it means people will see and sense their community. Not only will social models provide a way to build in resilience, they could enable a deeper connection to community in which we are creating. The next big ideas, the next big companies, or the next business models won't be created by those who say that what we already have works well enough.

The way we create value and the business models need to be reinvented. *Perpetually.* We may not yet have *all* the metrics we need to fully understand how, and who is winning, and by how much. But what's more important is to recognize that we're in a new game.

8. Unlocking Talent

Leading in a Social-Era world will require a new approach. Just as creating value has new levers, so does leadership.

Where the industrial era is oriented around the institution and its ability to create scale, the Social Era is oriented around how to formulate value with and by connected humans. This new orientation is changing how we value the individual and how we lead. Gazelles will choose where and when to assemble, based on where they will be nourished. So what needs to change? And what are the shifts in organizational practices?

Celebrating Onlyness

The first step is celebrating something I've termed *onlyness*. Onlyness is that thing that only that one individual can bring to a situation. It includes the journey and passions of each human. Onlyness is fundamentally about honoring each person: first as we view ourselves and second as we are valued. Each of us is standing in a spot that no one else occupies. That unique point of view is born of our accumulated experience, perspective, and vision. Some of those experiences are not as "perfect" as we might want, but even those experiences are a source for what you create. For example, the person whose younger sibling has a disease might grow up to work in medicine to find the cure. The person who is obsessed with beautiful details might end up caring about industrial design and reinvent how we all use technology. The person who has grown up under oppression might end up advocating for freedom of speech and thus advance the condition of his country. This individual *onlyness* is the fuel of vast creativity, innovations, and adaptability.

Embracing onlyness means that, as contributors, we must embrace our history, not deny it. This includes both our "dark" and our "light" sides. Because when we deny our history, vision, perspective, we are also denying a unique point of view, that which only we can bring to the situation. Each *onlyness* is essential for solving new problems, as well as for finding new solutions to old problems. Without it, people are simply cogs in a machine—dispensable and undervalued—and we're back to the 800-pound gorilla approach. With it, gazelles are singularly unique and able to contribute meaningfully.

It's not that everyone *will*, but that anyone *can*.

Some people, when we start talking about "unlocking all talent," roll their eyes and ask who would pour the coffee or stock the shelves in this new world. Well, let's look at an example where people are literally pouring the coffee. Every time we walk into Starbucks, something amazing happens without most of us really noticing. It is this: every staff member from the order taker to the café barista manages to make full eye contact with every customer. That signifies something. When people feel seen, valued, and respected, they can see, value, and respect. Starbucks has a long history of providing health-care benefits, decent wages, and a cultural norm of dignity as it prepares its 200,000 employees to do work. It trains people who come from a wide variety of backgrounds, sometimes from families that have no history of knowing how to organize their lives and get to work on time. It does more than instill procedures; it unlocks self-worth and personal dignity. That effort shows up the small ways we don't notice (eye contact), but also how we as consumers experience something in totality. Think of the comparable that does not instill a sense that everyone counts: Walmart, where people are largely treated as replaceable parts.

Now you could argue that Starbucks has higher margins where Walmart does not, but I would argue that the margins reflect the value created in and by the organization by its approach. Starbucks says everyone can contribute in a meaningful way, and then people do. One is a precondition of the other, not a by-product of the other.

While organizations have honored the gem from Jim Collins to get "the right people on the bus," once those people have been hired, too many organizations often ask them to sit down, shut up, and let someone else drive.[1] In chapter 1, the obituary for traditional strategy, I mentioned that the predominant way we've handled strategy was to focus on getting *the idea* right. This is necessary, but not sufficient. Implicitly, then, shifting from merely "thinking right" to "doing right" is key in the Social Era. Let's talk about what that looks like in practice.

In most organizations, one small group creates or "owns" strategy, and another much larger part "owns" execution. Across industries and countries, research shows only 5 percent of people know the strategy in an organization.[2] When only 5 percent of the people in an organization knows the strategy, then only 5 percent are ready to make decisions that align their work to that vision. It means only 5 percent are able to apply themselves to building that strategy into reality. Typically, this means that a part of the organization develops a great idea that is only fully understood in a small corner of that company. The larger organization then gets to work on the execution plan without ever really owning the strategy. While the strategy-execution gap is a persistent bugaboo, it becomes nearly catastrophic in the Social Era: you can't be fast, fluid, or flexible if 95 percent of the people in your company have no idea what direction they're supposed to be running toward.

This strategy-execution gap creates an "Air Sandwich"—an empty void in the organization between the high-level strategy conjured up in the stratosphere and the realization of that vision on the ground (let alone owned by anyone outside the organizational perimeter). The filling in

---

[1] Jim Collins's brilliant ideas are too often referenced out of context. I believe he meant that the quality of the "who" precedes delivering on the "what." In my eyes, who you are is what you make, which means we need to connect the people we engage to do their best.

[2] According to Robert Kaplan and David Norton, the creators of the *Balanced Scorecard*, http://blogs.hbr.org/hmu/2010/06/making-your-strategy-work -on-t.html, one practical idea every firm could do to improve their performance is to track and then improve how many of their organization know the direction of the firm.

an Air Sandwich consists mainly of misunderstandings, confusion, and misalignment, rather than the effective connections between the vision and the on-the-ground, fast-changing reality that make a good strategy a reality.

The Air Sandwich exists any time different participants lack a clear, shared understanding of the big picture. Usually, executives try to address it by working on their "communication skills."[3] But in practical terms, even a good communication plan does not create what is necessary: individuals to think through things enough to prepare to make the one thousand little decisions that are essential to make change really happen. When people are not involved in the formulation of a direction, they can never make it reality.[4] What needs to change is not the CEO's ability to communicate, but the premise that strategy creation can be separate from the people who will execute it. The Air Sandwich prevents us from reaching the desired end.

Strategy as a separate concept from execution is a relic of the past. It is something that was created when organizations needed structure to direct people who didn't have much education, where information was limited, and when markets and competitors moved slowly. In a world where we increasingly outsource or mechanize repetitive work, in which we've unlocked the free flow of information and built teams of highly educated millennium-generation talent that demands a seat at the table, we need to shift our approach from *telling* the strategy to co-creating it, so that it is owned throughout the organization.

Granting Power

The second step toward unlocking talent is establishing a baseline of shared understanding. The third is to allow people to make decisions. Those are, of course, linked in practical application.

---

[3] In *Execution: The Discipline of Getting Things Done*, Larry Bossidy and Ram Charan say that the problem with strategy is those darn employees; if only you could communicate things better, than the gap would be closed.

[4] My first book, *The New How*, (published by O'Reilly in 2010) was on the concept of the Air Sandwich and how to address this gap within organizations by collaboratively setting direction.

A case study brings this idea into practice. Google reveals its high-level direction to everyone who works there. Everyone is expected to know what matters to the company. The high-level direction is posted on an internal website and updated whenever it needs to be changed (not just quarterly or annually), petitioned by anyone. It is live to every employee regardless of level. Google actually treats its talented, principled, creative people like talented, principled, creative people, instead of brainless sheep. Google acknowledges that direction will constantly change, and it is every person's responsibility to align his or her work, to define the substrategies of product lines and markets, and to be adaptive.

At a minimum, posting the high-level strategy for everyone signals something important: we value your brain. Giving people this understanding unlocks them to truly show up, engage, and participate. Indeed, it actually demands something from them also. It says that everyone—not just the executives—is responsible for figuring out what and how his or her stuff fits into this big picture. At meetings, product managers are often asked the question, "How does your idea (project, product line, proposal, etc.) fit into the big picture?" The ensuing dialogue creates understanding. Understanding unlocks people to recognize what they need to let go of or change to shift from the current "here" to a new "there."

Google doesn't get everything right, but this transparency of direction, openness to change, owning responsibility for knowing the direction, and constantly asking everyone to align his or her daily work is how you unlock talent. These actions align us, letting us work together better, tighter, and faster. It's like the difference between the performance of driving on the Interstate 5 and the Indy 500.

This also recognizes the role each of us has in providing something: our onlyness. The Beatles famously did this for each other: John kept Paul from being a teeny-bopper, and Paul kept John from drifting out into the cosmos, while George lent soul to both. (I have to admit I can't explain Ringo's onlyness except to say that drummers are important.) The Social Era is ultimately about the way connected individuals form an ensemble and create value together.

From Knowing the Right Answer to Getting to the Right Outcome

Physics has a concept called the Heisenberg Uncertainty Principle. Werner Heisenberg says we can know either momentum or position, but not both. It seems to me that this applies to our organizations today. We can fixate on having a particular idea right (traditional strategy), or we can focus on the way in which people *engage* ideas so that we develop momentum and turn our intentions into outcomes.

After twenty years of being inside, advising, and running organizations, I've come to realize that all organizations are made up of conceptual boxes. Which boxes are our competitors in? Which ones are our customers in? Where do we fit on the org chart? Which building will we sit in, what title do we have, who is responsible for the budget?

Boxes can help us define what everyone is doing. That was especially helpful when things didn't change very fast; in those days, if we could confirm that everyone was doing the right thing today, then we could have some confidence that they would be doing the right thing tomorrow as well. But today, conceptual boxes do not help us achieve success.

That's because as soon as we make those boxes, we make something else too: space between the boxes. That space is always where things start to fall apart as our environment changes. While each of our roles matters, what matters more is the way those roles interact and engage with shared ideas. When we focus on boxes—as traditional organizational design work does—we try to keep people out of the spaces where failure happens. Back when things moved slowly, maybe we could get away with it because we had time to notice when little things would begin to unravel.

But firms that embody momentum are focused on how to take action. Firms that embody momentum are focused on how they think and act together. And this sets a pace or rhythm for work. When we embody momentum, our work is more fluid and resilient, more like a living, breathing organism that adapts to the world, where different limbs naturally move in concert.

Companies that focus on momentum have high personal ownership and incentives not just for personal achievement but collaborative achievement. Success isn't about how smart or good or accomplished any individual is (although, of course, that does matter), but in the resulting outcomes of what happens when all those talented individuals are in community, co-creating, with shared purpose.

Often at this point, some executives challenge me by saying, "This is the kind of feel-good message that doesn't translate to the real world!" Maybe you're thinking the same thing. We honor the things we can track and measure more easily than this seemingly "soft" stuff of people and leadership.

But, this approach to strategy and execution is well supported by empirical data. Gallup, the research firm, recently did a meta-analysis across 199 studies covering 152 organizations, 44 industries, and 26 countries. It showed that high employee engagement uplifts every business performance number. Profitability up 16 percent, productivity up 18 percent, customer loyalty up 12 percent, and quality up an incredible 60 percent.

These gains are based *just* on high employee engagement, the first (almost micro) step on the road from traditional strategy to the talent approach needed in the Social Era. Imagine what happens when direction is fully known, when insights are gathered everywhere and acted on quickly, when ownership is shared, when power is distributed. And these are not technically hard to do: share your direction, ask people to weigh in, allow for self-organizing teams rather than functional assignments, and so on. But it does require a level of comfort with uncertainty because it will seem messier to think of things in this way. And I say, "seem" because in reality, people working together is inherently messy and any tidy boxes we draw is not actually changing that situation, only the appearance of it.

Beyond the numbers, there are other benefits when we activate people to be fully alive at work. If you've been lucky enough to lead people when they fully contribute what they have to give, you'll know that this is when they are also their happiest. This is powerful. Back when we wanted brainless sheep for workers, and we could measure their output by, say, number of windows installed on a car assembly line, maybe we didn't need happiness. But now, people are working on trickier stuff. Happy workers solve problems over the weekend or in the shower, or wake up at 3 a.m. with breakthrough answers. This is the picture of a Social Era team.

Unlocking talent is not the frosting on the cupcake as it was in the industrial era. In the Social Era, it's the key ingredient in how we make the cupcake itself, and whether the cake is viable. Whereas the gorilla was about having the right strategy and having a few people own the direction, gazelle work is about distributed ownership where talent at all levels is unlocked to contribute onlyness and bring value in working together. When someone proposes that we can put off that talent engagement stuff until later, we can all answer with a resounding, "No, we can't."

9. Social Purpose

There are the things that we *do*.

There are the things that we *care* about.

And then there is the *story* we tell about it.

When those things are in full alignment for individuals, we say they have *integrity*. When we see them aligned in organizations, we honor their "brand" and "vision."[1] There is power in purpose, vision, and brand. On this theory, everyone can agree. An organization's purpose allows people to connect emotionally, it creates relevance in the marketplace, and it provides the direction for what to do next.

Purpose is arguably what distinguishes successful businesses with exponential impact from the rest. Too many 800-pound gorillas implicitly defaulted to "make a buck" as the thing they cared most about within the walls of the enterprise, but then told a different story to create market

---

[1] David Aaker taught us thirty years ago that branding isn't the stuff you tell in a story, but the way you have a story of something so unique that you end up creating your own category. It is the way we communicate the story we live. Jim Collins taught us that the best leaders care about the ambition of the cause rather than themselves, pointing to the need to care about purpose. Barry Posner and Jim Kouzes (the #1 leadership authors in the world) have thirty years of research encouraging leaders to bring out the best in people by engaging with purpose. Purpose is the deepest asset a firm can have in performance. But it reaches beyond brand and leadership. The Social Era lets purpose be the core asset from which to build the entire shebang.

relevance. The Social Era has raised the visibility of this gap between what organizations do and the story they (try to) tell.

In the early industrial era, purpose was often not shared throughout the organization. Management had an us-versus-them relationship with labor, with suboptimal consequences. Trade unions formed to bargain and continued the adversarial relationship. During the later "enlightened" years of the industrial era, firms realized the benefits of identifying a shared purpose that could engage all their employees and avoid the us-versus-them trap. Now in the Social Era, we need another term for the kind of purpose that reaches beyond the firm's hierarchies and silos. I'll call that social purpose.

Social purpose matters to the bottom line in three ways.

1. **Community**. As I discussed in chapter 4, work is freed from jobs. The reason someone might work with you is because of a shared goal. The shared purpose of "ideas worth spreading" appeals to and enables the TEDx community to magnify TED's impact a thousandfold. A purpose creates enthusiasm for work that needs to be done. The Nuru Project—a marketplace for photojournalism—puts purpose at the heart of its business model: 50 percent goes to nonprofits and 25 percent to the photographer. Purpose is magnetic in a way money alone isn't.

2. **Speed**. Imagine if every single person working with you understood the whole master plan and could use it as a decision-making yardstick. Small, medium-sized, and even big decisions would be better decided if everyone knew the big picture. In the Social Era, the power to make decisions doesn't come from your spot on the org chart, or rank, or any fancy-schmancy title. Power to make decisions comes from knowing which ideas matter to the organization and why. This clarity of purpose becomes the connective tissue to how value is created. Instead of being told what to do, you already *know*. When people *know* the purpose of an organization, they don't need to ask questions of swamped managers before taking the next step; they can just do it. Actions are aligned regardless of where someone—in or out, up or down—belongs.

3. **Relevance**. Meaning and relevance can be built into what market you serve and how you go about doing your work. This is fuzzy stuff, so here's an example to bring it home.

Have you ever walked into Sports Authority? In the United States, it's one of the biggest sporting goods retailers, with about four hundred stores. You can go in and buy just about anything from kayaks to tents to soccer gear. It carries major brands like Nike and North Face. But despite its name, experience shows that very few of its employees are authorities on the products they sell. Interacting with employees is almost painful; ask them a question and, after giving you a blank look, they simply read the same garment tag that you read before you flagged them down. They might do retail, but they don't seem to do sports. When everything is available online—with full specs, user reviews, and price comparisons—why make a trip to a store where you can't get any answers?

A trip to REI offers sharp contrast. That gal showing you which backpacks could work for your body type and journey will also ask you where you plan to go and then walk you over to show you the map that she used last weekend, pointing out the perfect lake and which side of that lake to camp on. You can tell that the people REI hires actually have a passion for sports and appreciating the outdoors. It holds clinics at no charge and encourages you to learn about the sport because the goal is to get you to do it, not just to buy the equipment for it.

The difference between the two organizations is this: one is selling sports-related stuff, and if it disappeared tomorrow, few beyond those who lost their paycheck would shed a tear. The other wants to get you to love sports; it has a set of strategic partnerships and ecosystems built around this vision, including programs to introduce city-bound teens to the woods, to push everyone who interacts with its brand to experience something bigger than themselves. An organization optimized to push product often sets up functions with distinct roles and responsibilities: one runs the cash register, another orders product. Customer loyalty can wind up as a function within marketing. But when an organization has a unifying social purpose, it overrides territorialism. Everyone owns the whole. In REI's case, this gives permission to teach about products and nurture enthusiasm; to advocate different vendors even if it doesn't stock them; to do research in time off to build a better understanding of outdoor sports. And because the goal is beyond the perimeter of REI's walls, community members will teach clinics at REI—even though they're not on the payroll—because they're drawn to its social purpose.

Through the years, as I've spent time exploring this topic of purpose, over and over I'm confronted with a **point of tension: purpose means different things to different people.** As I speak, people will nod their heads in agreement. Only later in conversation will we discover that we have very different meanings for *purpose*. We're using the same word, but we're not quite talking about the same thing. Many of you may prefer the terms "vision" or "mission" or "brand" instead of social purpose. If so, please understand that I'm not dogmatic about the term. Use whatever word works for you. What is important is an organization that manifests a broadly shared combination of meaning and relevance and does so in a way that aligns all parties.

One question I am often asked: how do you know if a purpose is good? I've noticed that purpose is often viewed as the *same* reason a business is in existence. That can be true. Yes, Sports Authority may think it has a purpose, but I argue that it doesn't have one that excites anyone outside the perimeter of the organization—which makes it more a goal of Sports Authority than a purpose of ours. It may have a "shared" purpose (within its walls), but it surely doesn't have a "social" one.

Social purpose gives our goals a "why."[2] Without social purpose, everything is procedural. Without the why, organizations rely on the *what*. As in, first we do this *what*, and then that *what*. When *whats* are the main course, work just becomes a series of tasks. A diet of *whats* relies on management assigning those tasks to make sure all the parts of the business are covered. Purpose shifts that. A shared purpose says that as long as you are clear on the goal, work with each other to get stuff done. Having a shared purpose allows power itself to be shared, for momentum to be built for stuff to happen without having to check back in. It builds fast, fluid, flexible into the very way you work. In that way, *purpose aligns*. Without it, you travel in circles, covering a lot of ground but not necessarily going anywhere because every action has to be directed instead of magnetically aligned from inside through reality.

---

[2] Someone who has done a great job packaging up this idea of "why" matters is thinker and speaker, Simon Sinek. You can see his TEDx talk on the topic— as 4 million others have—at http://www.ted.com/talks/simon_sinek_how_great _leaders_inspire_action.html.

A static organization with captive employees that is just doing more of what it did yesterday can do without a shared purpose. An organization that doesn't value community can use shared purpose while ignoring the idea of social purpose. But an organization that wants to engage with others, operate in changing times, and enable talent will find that its social purpose is essential to sustained health.

Tim O'Reilly, the publisher of my first book, once said that companies should do work that matters and let the rest take care of itself.[3] It seems to me an act of confidence (and perhaps even more deeply, faith) to believe that if you get the big picture right, you will build an organization that thrives. Whereas traditional strategy said you had to define each strategy right, the Social Era says get the big picture right and the rest takes care of itself. But this taps into a more fundamental truth: people crave meaningful work. Your ability to orient everything around a purpose will be the way you create exponential value.

---

[3] My favorite encapsulation of Tim O'Reilly's ideas can be found at http://radar.oreilly.com/2009/01/work-on-stuff-that-matters-fir.html.

10. Openness

One underlying value pervades much of what I have covered thus far—openness. Since it is so fundamental, I want to address it straight on. Openness is more than the stuff of open source. Openness is a stance—to share, to collaborate, to distribute power to many. With openness, the future is going to be co-created. Whenever we want something bigger and better, we need to be able to let go so that someone can build on what we've started.

Openness can be seen in the world today on societal, organizational, and personal levels. We recently saw this on the world stage during the Arab Spring. We see it in organizations when global brands like TED decide to open up with TEDx. And at the individual level, we see it in social networks and blogging.

Some would argue—me among them—that openness is the ethos of the social era. Organizations that focus less on setting up turf walls and more on being flexible end up being able to leap from opportunity to opportunity. They might sacrifice near-term profit optimization, but they get long-term prosperity and resilience.

Instead of holding an idea in a closed fist, hold it out in your open hand. Someone can see or understand ideas held in a fist only in the little parts visible between your clenched fingers. An open hand gives your idea space to get bigger. Held in an open hand, treated like a living thing, it can grow, it can spread, and it can be picked up by others and made into something that will touch many lives.

But others—perhaps you—suggest that openness is just a phase and philosophy of the young and unaware, something that people will grow out of.

After all, it's human nature. Anytime we give birth to anything—kids, companies, ideas—the natural instinct is to hold that thing close, to protect it from the big, scary world and the bad things in it. This is understandable, especially with kids. But should we do it for companies and ideas? Yes, protecting intellectual property (IP) in a closed system has allowed many a company to keep its edge. And of course, it used to be possible to erect barriers to entry from competitors and to establish entirely new markets that could be all yours.

And that's the key; it *used to work* when the rules of the industrial era were in place. Not so much in the Social Era.

To be sure, openness means letting go. But it also means making money and having power.

Perhaps the best example of this shift is Apple unlocking the software development kit (SDK) for the iPhone. From its earliest days, Apple always kept a tight rein on the experience; no third-party developers, no licensing of its operating system. But does anyone think the iPhone would have been as successful—with over a billion apps downloaded—if it hadn't moved its IP to an *open* model with the world? Anyone who doesn't like the walled-garden approach of Apple feels drawn to the open platform that is Google. And one could argue that the Android/Google *entirely* open strategy has lent success to that platform, now contributing to 50 percent of all the units in the world in a short four years. One can easily say that the openness of Android forced Apple to innovate faster, and thus the whole market improved. Openness also distributes wealth. Revenues used to flow to a few control points in the mobile world, the operators. With openness, revenues flow to a wider base of developers.

Openness fueled growth.

Yet, and this is key, it's not that everything is open, but that what needs to be, is. Each company had to get clear what parts of its platform it would hold tightly and what it would open up. The same could apply to democratic governments or leadership at any level; it's not that *all* things are open; participation has some rules to enable order, not chaos.

So I've proven the point that openness can lead to market power and profits. But you can't measure the impact of *openness* in that dimension alone. The implications must be understood systemically. Just like riding a bicycle builds muscles to help you to do more than ride a bicycle, openness creates strength beyond the direct impact.

While the Apple App Store only contributes 6 percent of the profits of the firm, it also empowers a developer ecosystem that helps drive adoption. And the more those developers are rewarded and enjoy sufficient benefits of this ecosystem; they are not advancing another approach. They form a first wall of defense for the one that is "open."

Also, openness allows people to move from wanting someone else to come fix their problem to being able to solve their own. For this, I'll move to a nonmobile story. A website called PatientsLikeMe was cofounded about ten years ago by three MIT engineers. The brother of one and friend of the others had been diagnosed with ALS (Lou Gehrig's disease) at the age of twenty-nine. As they began searching worldwide for ideas that would extend and improve the person's life, they built a health data-sharing platform that allowed patients to manage their own conditions, change the way industry conducts research, and improve care. Unlike most health-care policies that worry about privacy, PatientsLikeMe focuses on openness. It believes that sharing experiences and outcomes is good. Why? Because when patients share real-world data, collaboration on a global scale becomes possible. New treatments become possible. Most importantly, change becomes possible. And ultimately this leads to the greater purpose: speeding up the pace of research and fixing a broken health-care system.

In this way, PatientsLikeMe shows us another lesson about openness. When you share, you can make something better for everyone. And, the real key is that an open approach can get to new and better ideas—and a lot more of them—faster, as a system opens up. Openness is about allowing anyone, anywhere to contribute—not the people you think "can" or even the people that you think "should," but from the abundance and diversity of many people's experiences. As each person stands in a place only she sees, she can bring her onlyness to solve whatever problem she sees closest to her.

This is the hallmark of openness: it strengthens not just the direct act, but the indirect acts of community, of speed to create new solutions, and certainly of new solutions to old problems. Those add up to the reasons why openness is important.

I wasn't always a believer in openness. I once ran right over other people because I wanted to be "right" more than I wanted to build an idea that became real in the marketplace. And I personally liked being in charge and controlling and telling other people what to do.

In my late twenties, I was responsible for running the revenues for a big division of Autodesk. I had a lot of responsibility for a $200 million division of a Fortune 1,000 company. As a result, I thought I was pretty big stuff.

While we were preparing a multiyear growth strategy that would ultimately go to the board, I had a disagreement about a budget spend. I wanted the dollars to be spent more on new customer acquisition and less on other marketing activities that were existing programs. My counterpart in the business unit directly responsible for this disagreed with my idea, believing it was important to maintain existing programs while expanding. First, we disagreed privately, then publicly. As each of us was in a place to lose face, we both wanted to win. Even though this person was a friend, I thought it was an issue of "choose the person or choose the goal." I chose the goal. I played the archetype of a smart, accomplished, results-oriented person with a corner office, so I did what a lot of know-it-all people do: I focused on being right *over* this person. I took the argument into the corridors; I lobbied others to point out the flaw in my counterpart's argument. I did some spin.

Today, I refer to that moment in my career as the equivalent of doing a corporate takedown—a kind of "stick your foot out so they'll trip" move only slightly elevated from third-grade behavior. I know I sound like the villain of this story. That's because I was.

Yet, I honestly didn't know another way. I felt it was my role to get the ball across the finish line and I was going to do whatever it took to get it done.

And get it done we did. The board approved our direction; then-CEO Carol Bartz called me in for a chat. I was psyched; it was clear I was going to get the "attaboy" for my super-heroic efforts. At first, it started out that way, as she pointed out that she knew what I did to get the ball over the finish line. She knew I did what it took to win. She trusted my calls, she said. She knew I would deliver. But, she pointed out, what I had also done was alienate the team. I realized I was in the wrong, but I rationalized, referring to our tight time lines. She pointed out that the way I went about winning meant that the team would not trust me the next time. Ultimately, they might not execute the plan because of the way I'd *held it*. While she was right (and I secretly knew it), I kept arguing with her about the goal being the goal, and the goal being about the right idea, decided on at the highest echelons of the organization and then executed.

I was fired not long after.

Over the years, I've come to be glad that I had such a spectacular failure. I can't put some tissue paper and gift wrap around this experience, and package it up to suggest this didn't happen.

I do shake my head at my old self. But I understand where these beliefs came from. They were rooted in industrial era thinking. After all, the 800-pound gorillas in the marketplace that focus on IP and lawsuits embody a similar set of beliefs: that it's all about being right, being big, and dominating a space by controlling things. It's all about power as a limited commodity, defined by your position on the org chart. That it is better to have power over others, rather than leave yourself vulnerable.

Openness offers something. On a personal level, it lets me create with others something that we jointly own. On an organizational level, it allows for many contributions to create a bigger outcome. At a societal level, it allows for the shift from what is to what will be, so that many voices can participate in solving old problems and perhaps even invent the future. Banking on openness is like saying you have hope in people to create.

I point out this frame because it is so easy for any of us to not realize that this frame changes our vantage point. I ask you to think about what frames you are using to view the world. Frames are simply windows to shape understanding. You may be drawn to one and repelled by the other, without even realizing it. But learning to apply different frames and appreciating the difference deepens our understanding. Galileo discovered this when he built his first telescope.[1] Each lens he added contributed to a more accurate image of the heavens. Successful people do the same. They reframe until they understand the situation at hand.

Openness is a frame that helps us understand the social era. After all, we can continue to hold ideas tightly, but we must realize that this means they can't become shared ideas. They remain alone, isolated, and separated so that they can't be built upon, refined, and shaped into something bigger. I know it feels as if we are protecting things when we hold them tightly in a closed first. Maybe we're even hoping that if we do hold them tightly *enough*, we'll create a diamond. But, it is an act of faith to be open—to expose ideas to the world. It says we are open to what happens next.

---

[1] This reference to Galileo and lenses to frame was borrowed from *Reframing Organizations*, 3rd ed., by Lee Bolman and Terrence E. Deal.

11. **Levers**

Since I began writing and speaking about my ideas, many people have publicly and privately asked, "Doesn't this just mean the 800-pound gorilla dies?" Sort of like brontosauruses before them, they are unable to outrun the asteroid that hit the earth. Certainly, the people in the start-up world, many of whom already embody fast, fluid, flexible attributes, believe that the established players are fated to die. But one can look at the history of the dinosaurs and see that not all of them did die. Paleontologists have suggested that they are actually all around us today, as birds.

Applied to today's gorillas, the analogy probably holds. The species that adapt to the changes in the environment faster will surely do better. What is less clear is what the species will become as they adapt. Perhaps the new model for a successful business should be "nimble." Or "flux." Or "humanized." Or "networked." Or "social." Frankly, while I have drawn plenty of distinctions and done my share of naming in this book, I find the search for names less than fruitful.

It matters much more to me that you act.

Exploring the Change Itself

I can't tell you how to adapt to these gazelle constructs; no book can. To adapt to changing times, each of us must first be open to exploring the change itself. I can ask you to consider what adaptation might look like for you by providing three exercises.

1. From Paid to Purpose-driven

In the Social Era, purpose precedes scale. And as I discussed in chapters 4 and 9—how we organize in the Social Era—shared purpose allows many communities to engage with us, without us having to invest resources in controlling their actions. When TED unleashed TEDx, it created a force multiplier. Shared purpose aligns people without coordination costs. This is true both "inside" and "outside" the organization. Purpose is also a better motivator than money. Money, while necessary, motivates neither the best people, nor the best *in* people. Purpose does.

Actionable exercise: Have the people you work with write down the purpose of your shared work. Then compare answers. Then ask, are any of these purposes something that would create a multiplier effect? Engage hearts and minds?

Hint: I think the measure of this exercise is whether you can define a purpose that you want to have happen even if your organization were to disappear. It's the compelling reason you work on something. What is that?

2. From Isolated Organizations to Communities

The Social Era will reward those organizations that understand they can create more value with communities than they can on their own. There are many types of communities:

- Communities of *proximity*, where participants share a geographic location. Craigslist is an example of maximizing value based on communities of proximity. Regus is an example of a way to make every "office" independent of physical place. How could you engage communities? It could very well be that instead of handling recruitment yourself, you could turn to the thirteen hundred co-working `locations` to ask who can best do X. Or perhaps you eliminate the need for a centralized HQ and distribute work to be closer to customers. Or you might find a way to share resources based on proximity. Certainly, Robin Chase's company Zipcar (and her more recent company doing peer-to-peer car sharing, Buzzcar) is an example of an organization doing this.

- Communities of *passion* that share a common interest (photography, moms, health, food, or books), which can inform new product lines. That seems obvious and just an updated form of what focus groups and surveys once enabled. But it can also be an organizing principle for who you hire and how you engage so that what you produce is an embodiment of the passions. Think of Evan Williams, the founder of Twitter, who wanted to enable connections based on content, and the early team that was similarly passionate. Or how Caterina Fake built Flickr by building social connections among passionate photography users. Communities of passion can inform what you choose to create but also be tribes in which to create value.

- Communities of *purpose* that willingly share a common task to build something (like Wikipedia), which will carry your brand and its offer to another level. I've used TEDx as an example throughout. But what is also possible is organizing communities so that what you make is based on who you are. A firm in the UK started a denim company near Wales. Cardigan is a small town of four thousand people in which four hundred of them used to make jeans. Before the plant shut down, they made thirty-five thousand pairs a week for three decades. Then one day the factory left town. But all that skill and know-how remained. So a small bunch of entrepreneurs decided that this group had ten thousand hours logged, so they would start a new denim company based on this shared talent. The people at Hiut Denim Company bring this shared purpose to their work, not only because they want to bring manufacturing back home—to their community— but to bring their skill to breathe new life into their community.

- Communities of *practice*, in which people share a common career or field of business. They extend your offer because it extends their expertise (like McAfee Maniacs). Guilds may very well undergo resurgence because they allow freelance individuals who share a practice (say of writing, user design, or finance) to showcase a portfolio of work. Certainly, Behance.net is an example of an online guild. But I can imagine ways for guilds across any field.

- Communities of *providence* that allow people to discover connections with others (as in Facebook), enabling the sharing of information, products, and ideas. People who worked together briefly or maybe met at a conference stay loosely connected but then can activate those loose ties when they need to. LinkedIn can be used to organize communities of providence. Twitter is the ultimate community of providence because it allows you to learn and discover what is going on in a community without having to know those in the community already.

Actionable exercise: Imagine that if you asked, you could get communities to co-create with you. What could you do together? What would be one way to try it out?

3. From Closed to Open

While management often pays lip service to the notion that good ideas can come from anywhere and everywhere, in practice there are "thinkers" who create strategies and designated "doers" who execute those strategies. But that only leaves an `Air Sandwich` in the organization, where debates, trade-offs, and necessary discussions are skipped. This Air Sandwich is the source of strategic failure. Instead of centralized decisions, we need distributed input *and* distributed decisions. We need to go from a closed, exclusive concept of who can participate to an open and inclusive approach.

Actionable exercise: Rather than making command and control a "bad" thing, discuss what areas need which controls. Then examine how more, if not most, areas and decisions can be distributed (and thus made radically more flexible). For the purpose of the exercise, say that you want 50 percent or 70 percent of all decisions to be free of permission seeking and check-ins. What would it take to get there?

A friend asked me whether the Social Era is about reinvention. Specifically, "I feel like I'm going through a major reinvention just so I can go through a major reinvention." Rather than viewing change as an exception, we can understand that it is a natural part of the organization's development. And rather than fighting it, we need to embrace it. It might help to look at this situation in a case study of banking.

In the last ten years, major financial tools have been created: for example, PayPal, a simple form of online payments; Kickstarter, which allows crowdfunding of projects; and Square, which can make anyone a "merchant." The point is that the banking industry continues to ignore all these as "anomalies." They resist and are bound by what Traditional Strategy taught them (that sustainable advantages are to be maintained, and stability is preeminent).

At the same time, Bank of America recently considered a \$5 fee so customers could get their own money via their debit cards because the bank had to find a way to fund all its retail storefronts. This suggests a tendency to try and make the world conform to its view. Banking and—by extension—Wall Street continue to treat these new social constructs as "inconsequential" rather than redefining how they could create value themselves. This suggests a certain blindness to understanding the changing situation.

And, if you were creating a "bank" today, you would likely ask yourself how to accomplish the transactions (deposits, withdrawals, financial management) of banking without the physical commitment of banks. You wouldn't try and do it all yourself; you would engage community. You might build on the idea as ING is doing with its café model, providing a hub within a local geography. You might code mobile banking apps, like the ones transforming finance in Africa. You might even reimagine what it is to lend money, and rather than fight peer-to-peer loan legislation, you might enable local and social lending, as offered by the Lending Club.

Adaptability is central to how organizations (and people) thrive in the Social Era. In psychological language, the key to adaptability and personal growth is *resilience*. In biology, the equivalent term is *plasticity*. In financial language, we use the word *liquidity* to measure how flexible we are, how able to withstand what happens to us. In organizational design, the term is *flexibility*. And that is what these levers I've just covered add up to. When we emphasize purpose, engage communities, and distribute decision making, we begin to stop *talking* about these ideas in abstract and actually begin to make our organizations *become* fast, fluid, and flexible.

These ideas—purpose, community, and openness—are value levers in the Social Era, and through them, organizations can change how they consider every part of themselves.

Instead of being the gorilla that keeps everyone out and maintain its turf, we can find ways to bring together a herd of gazelles and be powerful by being nimble.

What Happens Now

Rather than try to power through with size, we'll have scale through community.

Rather than hiring and directing inside the walls of an organization, we'll tear down those walls altogether and allow everyone to own a part of the big picture.

Rather than taking long stretches of time to perfect something, we'll build fast, fluid, and flexible approaches.

What we create in the end will be a different type of organization, one that embodies a culture of constant innovation.

The picture of where we're going is still developing. But the fundamental principles of the Social Era are already clear enough for action now. We can recognize a new set of organizing principles. The world has changed; how we create value has changed. Organizationally, we have not. And it's time to do so.

The people who will change our world to be more connected, more purposeful, and more powerful—they are you. And it's time to start right now to reimagine how we're going to get a new kind of performance—for our organizations, our economies, and ourselves.

Acknowledgments

Whoever said writing was lonely, lied.

This book has been social in every way—from the board meeting that first inspired me to write down which ideas should be deemed passé to the vibrant discussions that evolved my first missives into more considered and complete ideas.

This includes an amazing tribe of people: Priya Parker, Julien Smith, Lisa Gansky, Bruno Giussani, Andrew Blau, Sameer Patel, Salim Ismail, Michael Mace, Harry Max, Tim Kastelle, Peter Sims, Michael Dila, Philip Auerswald, Haydn Shaughnessy, Ray Wang, Jennifer Aaker, Jimmy Guterman, Jean Russell, Sara Roberts, Whitney Johnson, Clint Korver, Alex Osterwalder, Les McKeown, Mitch Joel, Tereza Nemessanyi, Seth Cargiuolo, Vala Afshar, Leslie Bradshaw, Om Malik, Mair Dundon, Ruth Ann Harnisch, Anand Giridharadas, Jerry Michalski, Steven Wright, Craig Donato, Pam Fox Rollin, Tony Schwartz, and June Cohen. Each of you made this body of work as cogent and clear as it is. Thank you.

To all the global organizations that let me share—and pilot—*11 Rules for Creating Value in the Social Era*, your good work and courage to let go of what is known and steer into the *un*known keeps showing up in your results—and the front pages of the *Wall Street Journal*.

Every author has a secret-agent type who makes *good* ideas into *great* ones. For me, that person is my editor, Sarah Green, at *Harvard Business Review*. As a fellow thinker, she has championed me and challenged me at all the right times. And I am blessed with an amazing agent in Carol Franco. Thank you both for getting me to this point. You are a dream team.

At its best, writing is as creative as it is communal and collaborative. At its worst, it is messy, nonlinear, and fundamentally difficult. When I'm writing, I have a persistent feeling that the perfect sentence or chapter lies just beyond what I've been able to create thus far, and that if I stretch just a little bit more, the work product will get better—maybe even be perfect. It is my inner circle who endures with me while I try to leave it all on the field, yet these same people also embolden me to get back to work when I am discouraged. I can always count on you: Julie Beckmann, Laura Strange, Tara Hunt, Terri Griffith, Christine Campbell, and Glen Lubbert. And there are two people without whose support this work would never have gotten done: my husband, Curt Beckmann, and our son, Andrew. With you, I feel anything but alone. With you, I am fully alive. You fuel my passion to shift the ways of creating value to allow *everyone* to be fully alive.